VICKERS
WELLINGTON

VICKERS WELLINGTON

PHILIP BIRTLES

Fonthill Media Language Policy

Fonthill Media publishes in the international English language market. One language edition is published worldwide. As there are minor differences in spelling and presentation, especially with regard to American English and British English, a policy is necessary to define which form of English to use. The Fonthill Policy is to use the form of English native to the author. Philip Birtles was born and educated in Croydon; therefore, British English has been adopted in this publication.

Fonthill Media Limited
Fonthill Media LLC
www.fonthillmedia.com
office@fonthillmedia.com

First published in the United Kingdom and the United States of America 2022

British Library Cataloguing in Publication Data:
A catalogue record for this book is available from the British Library

Copyright © Philip Birtles 2022

ISBN 978-1-78155-868-3

The right of Philip Birtles to be identified as the author of this work has been asserted by him in accordance with the Copyright, Designs and Patents Act 1988.

All rights reserved. No part of this publication may be reproduced, stored in a retrieval system or transmitted in any form or by any means, electronic, mechanical, photocopying, recording or otherwise, without prior permission in writing from Fonthill Media Limited

Typeset in 10.5pt on13pt Sabon
Printed and bound in England

Contents

Introduction 7

1	Design and Development	9
2	Early Wellington Operations	39
3	Main Force Operations	75
4	Aircrew Training	95
5	Wellingtons in the Mediterranean	114
6	Maritime Operations	144
7	Asia, Africa, and Arabia	170
8	Multi-role Wellingtons	178
9	Post-War Service	195
10	Foreign Air Forces	207
11	Preserved Wellingtons	209

Appendix I: Specifications 217
Appendix II: Production 222
Appendix III: Service Units 226
Further Reading 236

Introduction

The Vickers Wellington bomber was one of the unsung heroes of the Second World War, being the most modern bomber available at the start of the war, and continuing in service into final retirement in 1955. Being a twin-engined aircraft, it was never going to be a strategic bomber and was overshadowed by its four-engined brethren—in particular, the Lancaster. Strategic heavy bombers capable of delivering a significant load into Germany, such as the Stirling and Halifax, were not delivered until February and March 1941, followed by the more effective Lancaster in March 1942.

However, the 'Wimpy' (as it was known) operated in a wide range of roles, including being part of Bomber Command in Britain right from the start; Wellingtons made the first bombing raid on Germany on the day after the Second World War started. It also supported Allied forces in the Mediterranean, followed by maritime operations mainly against the scourge of the U-boats on the North Atlantic convoys, sinking twenty-five U-boats. Wellingtons served on bomber duties in India and Burma against the Japanese, in the Middle East and Africa, and with Allied units. They were adapted as interim transports with armament removed, used on trials, for experimental and development work, for troop-carrying, glider-towing, and after the war as navigator aircrew trainers.

Wellingtons were the only RAF bomber to serve in its original role from the start to the finish of the war, operating in every major theatre. Wellingtons were part of the first combined bomber raid on Berlin, together with Whitleys. More than half the bomber strength used on the first 1,000 bomber raid in May 1942 consisted of Wellingtons, many from operation training units (OTUs) with instructors and aircrew under training, giving the novice crews early experience of combat; the target was Cologne. The total number produced was 11,462, which was around 50 per cent more than Lancasters at 7,366, and nearly double Halifax production at 6,176.

At its peak of operations in the autumn of 1942, there were sixty RAF bomber squadrons and OTUs equipped with Wellingtons, flying a total of around 47,500 combat operations for Bomber Command for the loss of 1,727 aircraft in combat and training. The longest-serving Wimpy unit was 99 Squadron, which introduced the type into RAF service in October 1938, operating for five and a half years. Wellingtons featured the Dr Barnes Wallis-developed geodetic construction with fabric covering, which was light and resistant to battle damage. The Wellington was overshadowed by the mighty Lancaster, like the robust Hawker Hurricane fighter in the Battle of Britain was dominated by the Spitfire. In the early stages of the war, the Wimpy was underpowered, but with new engines, its performance and reliability was significantly improved.

1
Design and Development

In the early 1930s, the RAF night bomber force was mainly still equipped with First World War technology biplanes, the Vickers Virginia being the most effective. However, the aircraft cruised at a mere 108 mph with a service ceiling of 15,530 feet and a maximum bomb load of 3,000 lb, which was a very little advance over the 1918 vintage Vimy that it replaced. Sharing in the bomber fleet were biplane and fixed undercarriage Handley Page Hinaidi and Heyford, while Fairey and Handley Page had designed the monoplanes Hendon and Harrow, neither of which had strong performance statistics.

The day bomber force was even worse off with only 101 Squadron equipped with the Boulton Paul Sidestrand, to be replaced by its development known as the Overstrand, with a maximum speed of 153 mph, a ceiling of 22,500 feet, but a modest load of 1,600 lb of bombs, over an inadequate range of 545 miles. In the 1920s, the natural perceived enemy of Britain had been France. With the growth of the German war machine in the 1930s, the government created the RAF Expansion Scheme, putting investment into permanent bomber stations in the belief that the bomber would always get through. There was little funding for defending fighter stations.

Following the failure of the Geneva Disarmament Conference in 1934, decisions were made to modernise the RAF, led by Chief of the Air Staff, Marshal of the RAF Sir Edward Ellington. As early as 1932, with an official recognition of lack of RAF bombing capability, Operational Requirement OR.5 was issued by the Air Ministry, specifying a twin-engined day bomber to replace the Sidestrand. On 20 October the same year, Specification B.9/32 was issued to the aircraft manufacturers with an invitation to respond, the need being to carry a bomb load of 1,650 lb over a range of 720 miles at a service ceiling of over 22,000 feet. The range could be increased to 1,250 miles using auxiliary fuel tanks, but this was hardly a major improvement over the existing bombers. The specification was also

B.9/32 Prototype K4049 on 950-hp Pegasus X engine ground runs prior to first flight. (*BAE Systems*)

part of RAF Expansion Scheme F, calling for replacement for all light bombers, an example being Hawker Hind biplanes, with medium bombers resulting in the Fairey Battle, Bristol Blenheim, and the slightly larger Armstrong Whitworth Whitley. Two manufacturers responded to B.9/32, and in February 1933, both were selected to produce prototypes—Handley Page with the Hampden and Vickers with their Type 271, later to become the Wellington in September 1936.

Design of the Wellington bomber was led by Rex Pierson, based on the Barnes Wallis-developed geodetic construction, and was a strong structure resistant to serious combat damage, allowing many aircraft to bring their crews home. Barnes Wallis had been involved in Britain's R100 airship programme at Cardington, and when the concept was abandoned in 1930 following the loss of the R101 at Beauvais on 5 October, he transferred his ideas in smaller scale to aircraft. Traditional aircraft construction consisted of a rectangle wooden framework structure with wooden stringers over which fabric was placed to give an aerodynamic shape, resulting in an overweight structure, much of which was redundant. Wallis created a new light alloy construction that had structural members forming the desired aerodynamic shape, produced in sections on assembly jigs. These bolted together without the need for heavy wooden beams and gave a roomy interior with a lighter, stiffer, and stronger structure, which was pre-formed to the required aerodynamic shape. This provided ample room inside the fuselage for systems and equipment, as well as in the wings for fuel tanks. While Pierson was responsible for the overall layout of the airframe, Wallis designed the structure, the first example being the single-engined Wellesley bomber.

Geodetic construction of the Wellington fuselage and wing centre-section. (*BAE Systems*)

Nacelle for Pegasus engine on stub wing. (*BAE Systems*)

The geodetic structure made use of a space frame formed from spiral crossing 'basket-weave' aluminium of load-bearing members. With the geodetic curves forming a pair of helices at right angles to one another, the members were mutually supporting with the torsion load on each cancelling out the other, giving a light, strong, and roomy structure.

The Wellesley was a general-purpose monoplane capable of bombing, reconnaissance, and army co-operation with a first flight in June 1935 in its prototype form. In its production form, it had a maximum speed of 228 mph, a range of 1,220 miles, and a service ceiling of 25,500 feet. The type entered service with 76 Squadron RAF in April 1937 with an overall total of 177 delivered. Three Wellesleys set a world distance record in November 1938, flying from Ismailia in Egypt to Darwin, Australia. When war was declared, although it was still in service in the Middle East, it was obsolete and finally withdrawn in 1944.

The same construction principles were applied for the twin-engined Wellington, which was the main RAF bomber at the start of the Second World War. The aircraft was commonly known as 'Wimpy' by the crews, after Popeye's friend J. Wellington Wimpy. The aircraft was powered in turn by Pegasus, Merlin, and Hercules engines mounted on the wings, which were midset in the streamlined fuselage. During the early part of the war, the Wimpy excelled as a night bomber, with the primary mission to destroy the German war machine during the hours of low light. With the entry into RAF service of more capable strategic heavy bombers, the Wellington became outclassed and more vulnerable to Luftwaffe night fighters. Wellingtons flew their final offensive Bomber Command mission in October 1943, but continued to serve with distinction in other roles.

Power came initially from two 950-hp Bristol Pegasus Mk X radial engines, and the first flight of B.9/32 prototype K4049 was made by chief test pilot Mutt Summers from Brooklands on 15 June 1936 for ten minutes. A second flight of twenty-five minutes was made the next day, and on 17 June, Summers flew the prototype to Eastleigh near Southampton, which was the centre of Vickers flight testing. Eastleigh was a much more suitable airfield, in comparison with the restricted space within the Brooklands racing circuit. The aircraft was flown back to Brooklands on 23 June to be prepared for the public debut at the Hendon Air Pageant on 29 June.

On 8 July, their royal highnesses the duke of York and the prince of Wales inspected the prototype in a line-up of a number of new fighters and bombers at Martlesham Heath. The prototype briefly visited the RAE (Royal Aircraft Establishment) at Farnborough before going back to the A&AEE (Aeroplane and Armament Establishment) at Martlesham Heath for Vickers heavyweight trials in November, ready for the official service performance and handling tests. There were some criticisms including poor workmanship, poor cockpit layout, and control difficulties, including a heavy rudder and excessive trim changes during overshooting.

With initial trials almost completed, the aircraft crashed on 19 April 1937 due to elevators breaking off, resulting in the death of the flight engineer, although the

Fuselage interior structure. (*BAE Systems*)

Pegasus engine installation. (*BAE Systems*)

Male and female labourers assembling fuselage panels. (*BAE Systems*)

B.9/32 Prototype K4049 made its maiden flight from Brooklands on 15 June 1936 by chief test pilot, Mutt Summers. (*BAE Systems*)

The B.9/32 Prototype had almost completed its initial development programme when it crashed on 19 April 1937 due to elevator failure. (*BAE Systems*)

B.9/32 Prototype K4049 in the new types park at Hendon on 27 June 1935. (*Newark Air Museum*)

pilot was thrown out as the aircraft broke up and came down by parachute. To prevent a similar occurrence in production aircraft, as part of the overall design development, a new fin, rudder, and elevator assembly was adopted.

Just two months after the first flight, a production order was placed by the Air Ministry on 15 August 1936 for 180 aircraft under contract number 549268/36, with further contracts following soon after, including one with Gloster Aircraft, which was subsequently reallocated to Vickers-Armstrong. The production standard was defined in Specification B.29/36 issued on 29 January 1936, with a bomb load of 4,500 lb consisting of varying sizes up to 500 lb, and the more powerful Pegasus Mk XVIII or Mk XX were fitted.

With anticipated volume production of all types of military aircraft, the government set up a shadow factory scheme in 1935, when large factories were constructed for mass production at dispersed sites around the industrial north and midlands where there was a plentiful labour supply. To cover the demands of producing Wellington bombers, a new factory was started at Broughton near Chester in November 1937. The first Mk I Wellington (X3160) was assembled from parts manufactured at Weighbridge, making its first flight on 2 August 1939. They started with an order for 750 aircraft, with a planned production rate of fifty a month. A second shadow factory was built at Squires Gate airport at Blackpool for Wellington production, with X3160 flying in August 1940, just a month before the factory at Weighbridge suffered an enemy bombing attack. The Blackpool factory was to produce 100 Wellingtons a month, but the Broughton factory built on the edge of Hawarden airfield was a much more comprehensive production facility featuring overhead cranes on tracks in the roof structure. There were also plans for de Havilland to operate a third shadow factory at Leavesden near Watford, but this was ultimately dedicated to Mosquito production.

The Broughton factory was the location where the Welsh workers took on the challenge of building a Wellington bomber in just twenty-four hours. German industry had a reputation for high efficiency in production, with the British being considered somewhat amateurs, but the Broughton workforce was prepared to prove that incorrect. The government was fully behind the plan, which would be good for morale and provide excellent propaganda. In co-operation with the RAF, the Ministry of Aircraft Production issued the challenge to factories producing aircraft for Bomber Command to beat the existing forty-eight-hour record claimed in California. In September 1940, Churchill declared that 'the bombers alone will provide the means for Victory', resulting in vast resources being allocated to the RAF.

The activity was set for a weekend in early summer 1943, the Broughton factory producing twenty-eight Wellingtons a week, with the factory still active now producing all the wings for Airbus airliners. The entire record attempt was to be filmed with a narrator from the Royal Canadian Air Force to project an American accent for the benefit of our Allies across the Atlantic, who joined the war well after it had started. Therefore on a Saturday morning in 1943,

Wellington final assembly at Brooklands. (*BAE Systems*)

Wellington Mk IC in final assembly. (*BAE Systems*)

Wellington GR XIV final assembly at Brooklands. (*BAE Systems*)

Wellington T X RP590 flying over the Blackpool factory, where it was built. This was the last of 11,462 Wellingtons and was delivered to the RAF on 25 October 1945. (*BAE Systems*)

Design and Development

The first Wellington assembled at Broughton with early nose gun turret. (*Newark Air Museum*)

A major shadow factory was built at Broughton near Chester, with Hawarden airfield alongside. (*BAE Systems*)

Broughton's workers—many of whom were women—commenced assembly of Wellington LN514 from scratch.

The factory at Broughton employed some 6,000 people, of which more than half were women, working to replace men called for war service. Many of them were responsible for stitching the fabric covering over the airframe, installing the electrical systems, and operating the overhead cranes that lifted the airframe assemblies into position. After the war, in the factory, de Havilland still used ladies to drive the cranes, sometimes lifting entire aircraft, such as a DH125 business jet, to a different position on the production line. Women played a vital part in aircraft production throughout the war, working in all the manufacturer's factories.

The assembly of LN514 started at 9 a.m., with the target to complete it in thirty hours and a pilot on standby to take it on its maiden flight. The metal assemblies were fastened together and the wings and fuselage joined with the two engines installed, all the time covering the metal skeleton with fabric at eight stitches to the inch. By 8.23 p.m., soon after the night shift arrived, the propellers were fitted to the engines, with the team ahead of their target. Two hours later, the 300-lb, 4.5-foot main wheels were installed, and by 3.20 a.m., the aircraft left the line to be inspected and made ready for engine runs, which were started at 6.15 a.m.—twenty-one hours and fifteen minutes since assembly commenced.

Engine runs were completed at 8.50 a.m., with ten minutes to go to the twenty-four-hour point and the aircraft ready to fly. The pilot had to be woken from his sleep as the workers had exceeded their work plan, the wheels lifting off the ground twenty-four hours and forty-eight minutes from the start. Later in the day, while the workforce continued to build Wellingtons, LN514 was delivered into RAF service.

An earlier aircraft produced at Broughton was Wellington Mk IC R1333, which was sponsored by the contractors, sub-contractors, and employees to the value of £15,000 and was delivered to 99 Squadron on 1 December 1940 at Newmarket. Unfortunately, 'The Broughton Wellington' crashed after take-off on 18 December and hit Devil's Dyke earthworks, killing both pilots and the rear gunner, but the front gunner and wireless operator were rescued.

Following the loss of the first prototype, it became a priority to continue the flight development programme, taking advantages of the lessons learned with the prototype, including an improved cockpit layout. The resulting first production aircraft had a revised fuselage configuration, incorporating provision for nose and tail guns and an improved tail layout. Mutt Summers took the first production Wellington Mk I L4212 for its maiden flight on 23 December 1937, checking general handling and controllability, the resulting flight test report being overall complimentary apart from some adjustments to the trim controls.

During the second flight, it was found that as speed increased, there was a severe oscillation in the control column. As flight testing continued, Barnes Wallis was often present as an observer, and by mid-January, the control oscillation had been cured with the fitting of balance weights.

Design and Development

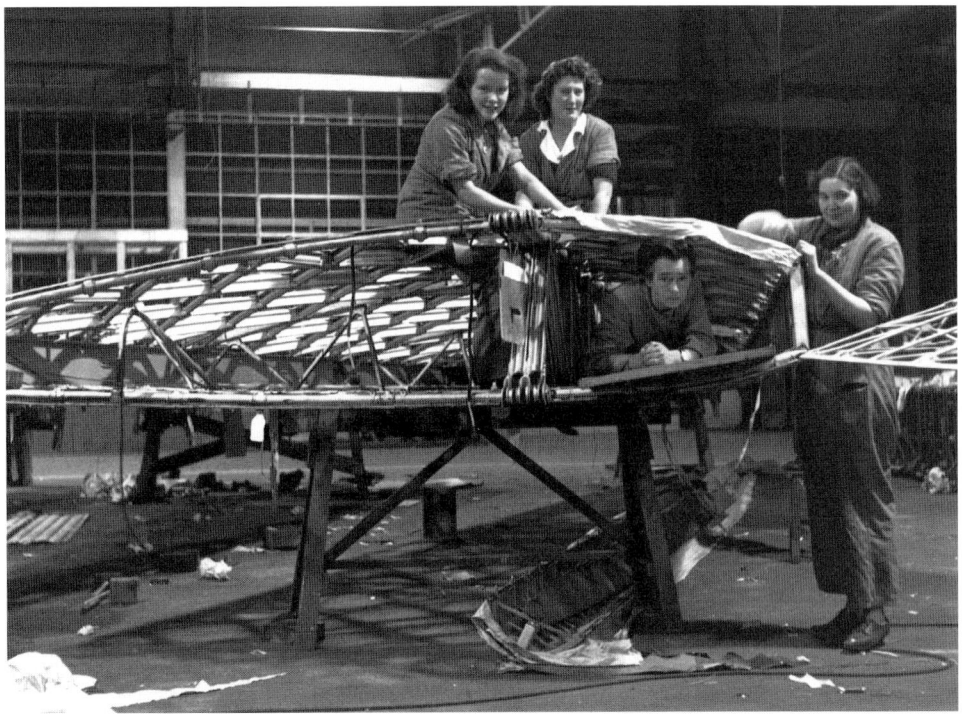

Female labourers covering a wing with fabric. (*BAE Systems*)

Female labourers rib stitching fabric to geodetic structural components before assembly. (*BAE Systems*)

Geodetic wing production. (*BAE Systems*)

Design and Development 23

Female labourers covering the front fuselage with fabric. (*RAF Museum*)

Wellington wing to fuselage assembly at Broughton. (*BAE Systems*)

First production Wellington B I L4212 powered by 1,050-hp Pegasus XVIIIs made its maiden flight on 23 December 1937. (*BAE Systems*)

Bomb doors were opened for the first time on 18 January 1938, and two days later, Air Inspection Directorate (AID) personnel were on board to assess the aircraft fitness for military use; the crew included Sqn Ldr Haines, the first RAF pilot to fly in a Wellington. With some seventy test flights completed by August 1938, the second aircraft (L4213) joined the flight development programme at Eastleigh, concentrating on landing and take-off performance at a modest load of 22,355 lb with a very short take-off run of only 333 yards and a landing speed of 79 mph. With criticism of longitudinal stability, ballast weights were fitted in the tail to stabilise the centre of gravity. The Pegasus XVIII engines were also tested, but at high power settings, the indicated air speed was lower than expected due to engines not maintaining boost.

The first Wellington was delivered to the A&AEE at Martlesham Heath in September for service trials. On the handling assessment, longitudinal stability was criticised, and when turning, the aircraft became close to the stall. It was noted the nose and tail gunners were not able to rotate with their guns, but this was later corrected. Armament testing shared with the tenth aircraft (L4221) achieved a bomb load of 4,500 lb but with a reduced fuel load. L4221 was also used for radio and electrical systems trials. Additional Wellingtons in the A&AEE fleet included L4213 for performance and fuel consumption development and L4217, which was fitted with dual controls in the cockpit.

With the rapid deteriorating political situation caused by the Munich Crisis in September 1938, Germany was permitted to take over parts of German-speaking

Czechoslovakia, which became known as the Sudetenland. This was by agreement of the major European countries as an act of appeasement towards Germany. As a result, re-equipping the RAF with new types of aircraft in development became urgent, with the Wellington being put into service before all the flight testing had been completed.

The first Wellington to enter service was L4215 with 99 Squadron at Mildenhall on 10 October 1938, replacing Handley Page Heyfords, with re-equipment completed over two months; the new type carried a bomb load of 4,500 lb over a range of 900 miles at a cruising speed of 180 mph. With the bomb load reduced to 3,500 lb, a range of 3,500 miles could be achieved. Defensive armament consisted initially of a Vickers K gun in the nose, two 0.303-inch machine guns in the tail, and a further machine gun in a retractable ventral turret. The five crew consisted of a pilot, observer/navigator, two radio operators/gunners, and one tail gunner; later, a second pilot was added. The crews were excited about operating this new aircraft with many modern features when compared with the types it was replacing. The pilots initially felt claustrophobic in the unfamiliar enclosed flight deck and were not used to its retractable undercarriage, which could easily be forgotten. The full instrument panel including an artificial horizon replacing the earlier elementary turn-and-bank indicator.

The 99 Squadron crews consisting of twenty officers and nineteen NCO pilots, many of whom were ex-Halton apprentices and were trained on the Wellington by Vickers at Brooklands. An initial three 99 Squadron aircraft were allocated to the Wellington development flight to conduct what was in effect service trials, determining fuel consumption and operational range, flying for up to nine hours; the total squadron strength was eighteen aircraft in two flights. As more aircraft were delivered, the original Parnall gun turrets were replaced by the more effective Frazer Nash turrets, the aircraft being designated Mk IA. Apart from regular oil leaks from the Pegasus engines, the Wellingtons remained reasonably serviceable, the major chore being fabric damage which was not easy to repair in all weathers, the total ground crew being about 110 personnel. In addition to maintaining the aircraft, the ground personnel had to maintain a duty crew, fire crew, and flare path detail, with the duty sergeant manning the flying control caravan. In addition, there was a Chance Light crew and guard duty, leaving little spare time.

The landing grounds were grass surface early in the war, and with night flying practice, the ground crew had to set out the goose-neck flares to designate the runway. The flare path crew normally consisted of a pilot, radio operator with battery-operated Aldis lamp, and ground crew to set out the flares in two lines for the aircraft to land between. The radio operator in the aircraft flashed the identification in green, requesting permission to approach, to which the ground-based duty pilot would send a green if clear to land or a red for an overshoot. The pilot then flew the line leading to the flare path, making wind corrections, aiming directly for where the ground party were standing, who had to get out of the way rapidly as the Wellington arrived.

No. 99 Squadron Wellington B I L4212 in 1939. (*BAE Systems*)

No. 99 Squadron Wellington B I L4212 with early nose gun turret. (*BAE Systems*)

The Fraser Nash turret-armed Wellington Mk IA was powered by Pegasus Xs; it featured soundproofing in the cabin, an astrodome for the navigator to take star sightings, and a fuel jettison system. It was recognised externally by having larger main wheels, which projected below the nacelles when retracted. The next Wellington version was the Mk II, which first flew on 3 March 1939 powered by Rolls-Royce Merlin Mk X engines; it flew before the Mk IA. This aircraft had a tendency to swing strongly to the left on full power take-off, which could be controlled by full right rudder and staggering the throttles. The Mk IC was powered by 1,050-hp Pegasus XVIII engines with the ventral turret replaced by two Vickers K or Browning machine guns firing from mid-fuselage positions. The final pre-war Wellington development was the Mk III, which first flew on 16 May 1939, powered by two 1,590-hp Bristol Hercules XI engines and fitted with a rear-mounted Frazer Nash four-gun turret.

The second unit to receive Wellingtons was 38 Squadron at Marham, replacing Fairey Hendons. The first Mk I (L4230) was delivered on 24 November, just over a month from the first delivery to 99 Squadron. The total replacement was completed by 12 January 1939. With production building up, it allowed seven more 3 Group squadrons to be equipped with Wellingtons, the type being declared operational for day bombing only.

In January 1939, IX Squadron at Stradishall replaced Heyfords, with 149 Squadron at Mildenhall also replacing Heyfords. In March, both 115 and 148 Squadrons received Wellingtons. In May, 37 Squadron and 214 Squadron both at Feltwell replaced Harrows, and 215 Squadron replaced Harrows at Honington in July. No. 115 Squadron was allocated to de-icing trials and blind-landing Lorenz system testing at night, which required a demanding standard of flying. On 1 June, a Royal New Zealand Air Force (RNZAF) flight formed at Marham to commence the operation of two squadrons with thirty Wellingtons ordered for operations from New Zealand, the crews having been sent to Britain for training before the war. At the outbreak of war, six Wellingtons had been delivered and the Marham Flight became part of 75 (RNZAF) Squadron, which formed at Stradishall in July 1939, becoming part of RAF Bomber Command.

During the pre-war months, training concentrated on close-formation flying to achieve mutual defence on daylight raids, yet this did not achieve the desired results. During the summer, the Wellington squadrons were tasked with flying low-level daylight practice, which appeared to be a change in the expected operational role. Training itself was not without hazards, and by 3 September 1939, when war was declared, six Wellingtons had been lost in accidents. The first was 38 Squadron's L4243 on 15 May, which was practising a shallow dive attack on Marham when an engine failed and caught fire. The pilot attempted a crash landing in a nearby field, but the aircraft was destroyed by fire, fortunately without loss of life. On 21 July, 148 Squadron's L4290, flown by a New Zealand pilot, suffered loss of control in cloud and crashed to the ground, killing the four crew.

Wellington B II prototype L4250 powered by two 1,145-hp Rolls-Royce Merlin X engines. (*RAF Museum*)

Early production Wellington B II L4252 with Rolls-Royce Merlin X power. (*BAE Systems*)

Rolls-Royce Merlin X engine installation in a Wellington B II. (*BAE Systems*)

Merlin X-powered Wellington B II T2545. (*BAE Systems*)

Wellington B IC P9242 powered by two 1,050-hp Pegasus XVIII engines. (*RAF Museum*)

Wellington B IC P9249. (*RAF Museum*)

Design and Development

Pegasus XVIII-powered Wellington B IC P9249 in 1940. (*RAF Museum*)

Hercules XI-powered Wellington B III L4251 being prepared by ground crew. (*BAE Systems*)

Wellington B III P9238, February 1941. (*RAF Museum*)

Wellington B I L4236 NH-R of Marham-based 38 Squadron. (*BAE Systems*)

Design and Development

Wellington B Is of Stradishall-based IX Squadron over France in 1939. (*RAF Museum*)

Wellington B Is of Mildenhall-based 149 Squadron, including LY-G. (*BAE Systems*)

Wellington B Is of Stradishall-based 75 (NZ) Squadron in formation during 1940. (*RAF Museum*)

Five Wellingtons were lost during August, plus an unfortunate ground accident. On 8 August, Air Commodore Arthur Thomson of the AOC 3 Group was carrying out live bombing practice at Larkhill when a hung-up bomb dropped out of the aircraft on the ground and Thomson jumped back into the turning propeller. On 9 August, L4258 of 149 Squadron went missing over the North Sea in bad weather with the loss of the crew. On 11 August, L4240 of 38 Squadron overshot in poor visibility at Debden, with a failed port engine, and hit a parked Hurricane before running into trees, but the crew survived. On 29 August, two Wellingtons were written off, with L4217 of 99 Squadron crashing on take-off from Mildenhall following an engine failure, but the crew survived with two suffering minor injuries and the aircraft was consumed by fire, and L4257 of 149 Squadron, which hit the sea in bad weather with the loss of the crew.

Preparations continued with training for combat. In February 1939, four aircraft from 38 Squadron attended the armament training camp at Acklington for a month's air gunner's training. In mid-March, the same squadron went on a dispersed exercise, living under canvas at West Raynham, although weather conditions reduced flying activities. In April, the squadron sent nine Wellingtons to Northolt for fighter affiliation exercises with the Air Fighting Development Establishment (AFDE) with exercises carried out by day and night, the latter for training searchlight crews. The night exercises were initially carried out near

Aldershot on pre-determined mock bombing runs, with patrolling defending fighters attacking any bomber illuminated by the searchlights. Daylight exercises were to assess the effectiveness of the mutual protection formations with a maximum of six Wellingtons either in two 'vics' or close box formation. The fighters approached from all directions, but the most effective for the fighters were attacks from the rear.

The first time multiple Wellingtons were seen by the public was at a display at RAF Northolt for MPs and guests on 23 May 1939, when a total of twenty-four flew over in formation. A week later on 30 May, the last Empire Day was held with seventy-eight RAF stations open to the public and all the aircraft painted in camouflage as part of the preparations for war. Wellington bombers were present at many of the stations either on static display or flying. Attendance numbers generally doubled from the previous year, signifying a public interest in the preparations for hostilities. Overseas visits included IX (Bomber) Squadron flying Wellingtons to the International Aeronautical Exhibition in Brussels held in July 1939, and 149 Squadron flying a formation over Paris in celebration of Bastille Day on 14 July. Exercises included dropping photo flashes over two target towns, followed by a low-level flight at 50 feet from the east coast to Leicester and Cheltenham by two flights of three aircraft on 13 July, with all aircraft reaching their designated targets.

Wellington B III 1,590-hp Hercules XI-powered prototype L4251 with Spitfire Mk I in 1939. This prototype first flew on 16 May 1939. (*RAF Museum*)

Wellington B Is of IX Squadron take off from Evere airport, Brussels, after visiting for the Second International Salon of Aeronautics in July 1939. (*BAE Systems*)

Wellington B Is of 149 Squadron, including Weybridge-built L4253. (*RAF Museum*)

With tension building, all units were ordered on 3 August to readiness level 'C' with effect from 11 a.m. on 7 August, meaning aircraft had to be available for operations at twenty-four hours' notice, all refuelled with armaments loaded and equipment ready. The next day, readiness state was raised to 'D', requiring all serviceable aircraft to be loaded with ammunition and pyrotechnics ready for operations, and the aircraft were dispersed around airfields with personnel wearing protective anti-gas clothing. A major home defence exercise was held over Britain from 8 to 11 August to test the readiness of all air and ground forces against enemy air attack. Much of southern and eastern England was involved with the friendly 'Westland' forces defending against air attack from 'Eastland' located across the North Sea. This largest exercise so far involved some 60,000 personnel and 1,300 aircraft, with friendly aircraft having white crosses superimposed over the roundels.

In command of the exercise was by ACM Sir Hugh Dowding, AOC Fighter Command. It consisted of around 800 aircraft, including 500 fighters and fifty reconnaissance aircraft. A force of 'friendly' non hostile bombers commanded by ACM Sir Edgar Ludlow-Hewitt, AOC Bomber Command, was included as a nuisance diversion, without any concept of the strategic use of bombers. The opposing 'Eastland' force, also commanded by Ludlow-Hewitt, had 500 bombers consisting of Battles, Blenheims, and Wellingtons, which overflew France the night prior before turning back to approach across the North Sea to simulate the 'Eastland' hostile force. In preparation, formations of Wellingtons had flown to Marseilles and back on navigation training, with the British and French public enjoying the low-flying formations manoeuvring over the countryside.

The crews were given a free opportunity in the planning and operation of the exercise to achieve maximum training results. If a fighter pilot believed he was in a good position to shoot down a bomber, he would indicate by flashing his recognition lights for a minute, with possibly a recognition return signal from the bomber. The bomber crews indicated their bombing run by illuminating their recognition lights. Both London and Southampton were designated as target cities, with London being blacked out in the latter raids. While new types of aircraft were being introduced to service, Bomber Command was preparing plans of how to use the aircraft once hostilities commenced. Following the 1937 Munich crisis, a list of targets in Germany was drawn up as part of the Western Air Plans for the destruction of the German Air Force, military communications, and industry as priorities. Luftwaffe airfields and supporting industry were targets, as were road, rail, and water communications to delay enemy advances, and industrial targets would be concentrated in the Ruhr Valley plus the supply of oil for fuel.

With the German invasion of Poland on 1 September 1939, the RAF moved on to a war readiness, which included Wellington units. An example was 99 Squadron, when the air and ground crews were ordered to collect their belongings and be ready within thirty minutes, for dispersal from Mildenhall to the rather austere Newmarket Heath racecourse around 10 miles away, some by air and others by road, commandeering some of the buildings. Some were sleeping under the grandstand canopy, in effect in the open, and food was served from a field kitchen. The officers were moved into the relative comfort of the Jockey Club, and the squadron had to provide support for eighteen aircraft dispersed in the open around the site.

Meanwhile at Marham, 38 Squadron also had eighteen aircraft, with twelve available for operations. Personnel included seventeen flying and pilot officers, ten sergeant pilots, sixteen sergeant observers, sixteen wireless operators, and ground crew of one warrant officer with fifteen flight sergeants and sergeants, seventeen corporals, and 145 airmen all under the squadron commander and two squadron leader flight commanders. Marham was a permanent RAF station, with the aircraft dispersed around the perimeter, but as it would be targeted by the enemy, the available twelve Wellingtons were dispersed to the rudimentary satellite at Barton Bendish, a large field 5 miles to the south-west of Marham. Tented accommodation was provided with gas clothing, identity discs, and small arms. No flying was attempted the next day to conserve the aircraft for operations, but overnight rain caused the airfield surface to become waterlogged, making it impossible to fly.

War was declared at 11.15 a.m. on Sunday, 3 September 1939, and 38 Squadron flew all its Wellingtons to South Cerney in Gloucestershire, with the squadron flying in line astern with basic crews, keeping away from other airfields. One aircraft had to force-land at Little Rissington with engine trouble. Other Wellington squadrons were dispersed similarly around England, to prepare for a long war.

2
Early Wellington Operations

At the start of the war, Bomber Command was ready to support Western Air Plans 1, 4, and 5, which targeted German military and manufacturing industry with six Wellington squadrons, as well as six squadrons of Blenheims, five with Whitleys, and six with Hampdens. All Fairey Battle units were deployed to France. Operational Wellington units were IX, 37, 38, 99, 115, and 149 Squadrons, with 214 and 215 working up to operational standard. Limitations were imposed by an appeal from President Roosevelt to avoid any operations that could cause civilian casualties, which in effect precluded any bombing of mainland Germany, leaving the only practical targets as enemy ships at sea or anchored in harbours, but not tied up alongside. With the combatants of both sides of the Atlantic in agreement, the only operations over Germany were reconnaissance and leaflet-dropping raids, resulting in what was known as the 'Phoney War', which remained in place until April 1940, when Germany invaded Denmark and Norway.

The Wellington force started combat operations on the first day of the war, 3 September 1939, with twelve aircraft from 37 and 149 Squadron from Mildenhall on an armed reconnaissance off Wilhelmshaven tasked to locate and attack enemy shipping in the North Sea. They had instructions to jettison their bombs in the sea if no ships were seen before dark. Nine Wellingtons reached the designated search area, but no targets were found and the aircraft returned safely to base. The next day, IX and 149 squadrons were again despatched to seek out and attack two enemy battle cruisers—the *Scharnhorst* and the *Gneisenau*—*en route* to the Kiel Canal. Fourteen Wellingtons were in the first wave. The first section was intercepted by nine enemy fighters and the other section experiencing anti-aircraft fire, but one ship was set on fire. With poor weather and light conditions causing navigation errors, bombing was spread out and some were inadvertently dropped on Esbjerg in Denmark.

Wellington B IA N2912 LG from 215 Squadron. (*BAE Systems*)

Wellington B IAs LG from 215 Squadron. (*BAE Systems*)

Wellington B IC OJ-W from 149 Squadron in January 1939. (*Newark Air Museum*)

Wellington B Is of IX Squadron. (*BAE Systems*)

A Wellington B I's bomb load. (*RAF Museum*)

Typical crew for a Wimpy ready for an operation. (*RAF Museum*)

No. 149 Squadron Wellington B IC L7813 OJ-R. (*RAF Museum*)

Unfortunately, two Wellingtons became the first losses of the Second World War, both with IX Squadron, one intercepted by a Bf 109 and the other by ground fire, both crews being killed. Soon after, IX Squadron began to replace its fixed turret Mk Is for the more effective Mk IAs, with eighteen being delivered by Christmas. The number of Wellingtons established on each squadron became twenty-four by January 1940. Following the raid, the squadron was deployed to Boscombe Down but returned to base after two weeks to continue training with the increased firepower.

The squadrons continued training in between operations, with frequent short-term deployments to other airfields; an example was 99 Squadron being called to the alert on 5 September and the next day was sent to Upper Heyford in Oxfordshire with eleven aircraft, only to have four return to Newmarket on 7 September for a leaflet raid, leaving the remaining aircraft practicing air firing at Carew Cheriton. On 9 September, it was decided to evacuate Newmarket, moving all the aircraft, including the ones still at Upper Heyford, to Elmdon airport, Birmingham. Five days later, the squadron was back at Newmarket. One Wellington was lost at Carew Cheriton when after an engine failure on take-off, during the attempted forced-landing, it collided with a Henley target tug.

It soon became apparent that when the expected hordes of German bomber attacks were unlikely to happen, the deployments stopped, allowing the permanent stations to provide full support to the planned operations. From its rearward base at South Cerney, 38 Squadron returned to Marham on 15 September. On 30 October, 99 Squadron made its first operation of the Second World War when the target was the German fleet off the Heligoland Bight, but it was abandoned due to bad weather, resulting in the target not being identified. With units receiving better support, the next significant operation was on 3 December when twenty-four Wellingtons attacked German warships, with hits claimed on a cruiser and no losses despite attacks from defending Bf 109s. Due to a bomb hanging up in a 115 Squadron aircraft, when accidently dropped on Heligoland, it became the first bomb dropped on German territory in the Second World War.

The charmed life for the Wellingtons ended on 14 December with a daylight bomber formation raid of twenty-three Hampdens, seven Whitleys, and twelve 99 Squadron Wellingtons. The unescorted formations were tasked for an anti-shipping patrol and located an enemy battle cruiser, a cruiser, and three destroyers in Schilling Roads, north of Wilhelmshaven in what was to become known as the Battle of Heligoland Bight. Due to a cloud base of only 200 feet, bombing was difficult and while loitering in the area, the bombers came under a sustained attack from Luftwaffe fighters and ground fire, with the loss of five Wellingtons and crews and no hits on the shipping. Of the seven Wellingtons that returned to Newmarket, only one was undamaged. In addition to four aircraft being shot down over the target, one Wellington had lost a flap, and when the remaining flap was lowered for landing, the aircraft rolled over out of control and crashed near the airfield. As a result of this disaster, Bomber Command strategy had to be changed since unescorted bomber daylight raids were too vulnerable to enemy defences.

On 18 December, only four days after the disastrous 99 Squadron operation, a repeat attack was made on the same target by twenty-four Wellingtons of IX, 37, and 149 Squadrons, but they were ordered to stay above 10,000 feet in the hope of avoiding the worst of the enemy's anti-aircraft guns. A number of German ships were located and bombed from 13,000 feet, but the use of ground-based radar-directed Luftwaffe fighters on to the bombers, and from the widely spread-out formations, resulted in twelve aircraft being shot down, five each from IX and 37 Squadron and two from 149 Squadron, with fifty-six aircrew killed. Soon after, ACM Sir Edgar Ludlow-Hewitt debriefed the surviving crews at Mildenhall and Honington.

AVM Arthur Harris, the AOC 5 Group, still believed that three or more bombers flying in close formation could successfully provide mutual defence against enemy fighters, and on 2 January 1940, three Wellingtons from 149 Squadron were tasked with a daylight reconnaissance of Heligoland Bight. While still 80 miles to go to the target, the formation was intercepted by Me 110s and two aircraft were shot down, with the loss of both crews, the remaining aircraft returning to Mildenhall. There was then an immediate order from the AOC Bomber Command that all Wellingtons and Hampdens were to only perform night operations. Wellingtons were also allocated to leaflet raids—termed 'Nickelling'—as well as night reconnaissance, commencing on 4–5 January. The casualty rate was significantly reduced to three Wellingtons lost during the next three months. Navigation was still highly inaccurate as flying had to be done by dead reckoning

Wellington B I of 38 Squadron on a waterlogged airfield in winter. (*BAE Systems*)

Wellington B III X3946 KO-Q from 115 Squadron ready for its next bomb load. (*BAE Systems*)

(DR) with unforecast winds and a lack of accurate landmark fixes. The radio and navigation aids installed in Wellingtons were primitive with a standard W/T transmitter and receiver.

A further unsuccessful attempt was made to locate the German fleet on the night of 20–21 February, and as a result of high-priority attacks on enemy naval shipping, another daylight reconnaissance was made on 12 April, when a fleet of thirty-six Wellingtons (together with Blenheims and Hampdens) flew over Heligoland Bight, but not surprisingly, fighter and anti-aircraft guns accounted for three Wellingtons and six Hampdens. Two of the Wellington crews survived by abandoning their aircraft or crash landing. This was the last RAF daylight operation for both types, and the restriction of not bombing German mainland was lifted, allowing Bomber Command to be more effective. An alternative method of catching the German fleet was to lay mines, commonly known as 'Gardening', which still had its hazards as the approach to release had to be at low level.

With European mainland bombing now permitted, military targets were a priority, particularly German-occupied airfields supporting the campaigns against Denmark and Norway. Among those attacked were Aalborg, Fornebu, Stavanger, and Sylt. The first of these attacks was by fifteen aircraft from IX and 115 Squadrons on 11 April when Stavanger was the target, although due to bad weather, only one aircraft dropped bombs on the airfield.

By the time 115 Squadron reequipped with Lancasters in early 1943, the squadron had lost a total of ninety-eight Wellingtons—more than any other squadron in Bomber Command. On 12 April, the largest bomber force of the war so far was despatched with eighty-three aircraft, including thirty-six Wellingtons making a daylight attack against German shipping in the invasion force against Norway. Ten days later, a flight of three Wellingtons was able to hit Stavanger airfield, followed by another successful attack on 23 May, when opposition was light.

All constraints on bombing the European mainland ended when Germany invaded Belgium and Holland on 10 May 1940, with Bomber Command targeting airfields, major road and rail networks, and communications in an effort to impede the enemy advance. On the first night, an attack was made on Rotterdam airport by a force of thirty-six Wellingtons, with further similar attacks building up during what became known as the Battle of France. In addition, on the night of 15–16 May, bombing a number of industrial targets in the Ruhr Valley commenced. With the enemy troops and armour rolling forward at gathering speed, the situation was becoming desperate for Allied armies, with Wellingtons, Hampdens, and Whitleys attacking from the air German troop concentrations, airfields, and communications in an effort to stem the advances. By the time the Battle of France was over on 26 June, a total of sixteen Wellingtons had been shot down, consisting of six from 99 Squadron, three from 37 and 115 Squadrons, two from 149 Squadron, and one each from 38 and 75 Squadrons—all the active Wellington units being involved, with the loss of many of the crews.

On 10 June, Italy declared war on the Britain and France, which was followed a few days later by a detachment of three Wellingtons from each of IX, 37, 99, and 149 Squadrons to Salon, Provence, for a successful attack on Milan and a second on Milan and Genoa without loss. These operations were without French co-operation, and an attempted third raid had to be abandoned due to the runway being blocked by vehicles, and the aircraft returned home.

At the height of the Battle of Britain in August 1940, the whole of Bomber Command was brought to full readiness with all leave cancelled, ready for operations against enemy seaborne invasion, which was expected at any time. All Wellingtons were loaded to their maximum capacity of eighteen 250-lb bombs. This did not mean the bomber fleet was sitting on the ground waiting, but they were targeting the invasion barge fleet in the channel ports, while also making regular sorties to Germany. This variety of operations kept the armourers busy, as if the Wimpys were allocated to normal operations, they would have to remove the 250-lb bombs and replace them with a mixed load of 500-lb bombs and incendiaries. On return from the sortie, the aircraft bomb load would revert to the anti-invasion standby configuration.

With Germany and occupied Europe now becoming available for strategic bombing, and new crews completing training, they were introduced to operational flying by flying leaflet raids. One of the early bombing raids was by 38 Squadron on 16 August on Hamm and Hamburg. On the night of 24–25 August, bombs

Wellington B III LN-F from IX Squadron, which force-landed in enemy territory and was captured with the crew taken prisoner. (*BAE Systems*)

Mildenhall-based Wellington B Is OJ-W and OJ-N from 149 Squadron in 1940–41. (*RAF Museum*)

Wellington B IA from 149 Squadron refuel and 250-lb bomb-loading at Mildenhall, 1940. (*RAF Museum*)

Wellington B Is WO-J from 149 Squadron. (*RAF Museum*)

Wellington B IA N2871 WS-B from IX Squadron returned from an operation with battle damage. (*BAE Systems*)

were dropped in error on London for the first time by the Luftwaffe, the intended target having been the refineries at Thames Haven. In retaliation, Churchill ordered an attack on Berlin the following night by a force of Wellingtons and Hampdens. Due to poor visibility, bombing accuracy was poor, but no bombers were lost and two more raids were made during the remainder of the month. The programme of strategic bombing of German cities was commencing, and Berlin was considered an easy target initially, but it became much more dangerous once the defences had built up by the following year.

During the Battle of Britain, Bomber Command was tasked with disruption of German industry and attacks on Channel ports to forestall Hitler's invasion plans, including the destruction of the fleet of barges being prepared. A major raid was despatched on the night of 14–15 September with forty-three Wellingtons, including 99 and 149 Squadrons, in a force of 157 bombers, and two Wellingtons were lost with their crews, in addition to six other bombers. The turning point of the Battle of Britain was 15 September, following which, due to Bombing Command attacks on Berlin, Hitler switched the attempted destruction of Fighter Command and airfields to the London Blitz. This removed the pressure on Fighter Command and allowed them to regain strength and eventually win the Battle. During the night of 17–18 September, 214 Squadron was part of a force of 194 bombers against the European Channel ports, one being Ostend, which had no flak defences. The port and railway installations were set on fire with damage to warships, and ten 214 Squadron aircraft were bombed without losses.

With the failure of the Luftwaffe to destroy Fighter Command, and due to expected winter weather in the Channel, Hitler turned his attention against Russia, his former ally, with the planned invasion of Britain to be the spring of 1941. Meanwhile, Bomber Command was expanding to undertake the increasing task of strategic bombing across occupied Europe. In October 1940, Wellingtons replaced Battles with 103 and 150 Squadrons, followed in November by Wellingtons re-equipping 12, 15, 40, 57, 142, and 218 Squadrons.

In addition to the regular RAF squadrons, Czech and Polish manned units were formed including 311 (Czech) Squadron, the first new RAF Wellington unit since 1939, at Honington on 29 July 1940 from Czech personnel, who had served in France before the German invasion. They were part of 3 Group going into action on the night of 10–11 September. They continued on bomber duties until late April 1942 when the squadron was transferred to Coastal Command on general reconnaissance duties. No. 311 Squadron had flown 1,021 operational sorties, dropping more than 1,300 tons of bombs; soon after joining Coastal Command, they went on the third 1,000 bomber raid, against Bremmen.

No. 301 (Polish) Squadron formed at Swinderby in August 1940 and began replacing its Battles with Wellington ICs in October, later converting to Wellington Mk IVs, continuing on bombing operations until disbandment on 7 April 1943, having flown 1,260 sorties, dropping 1,428 tons of bombs and 222 tons of mines, with a total of 203 aircrew killed, missing, or taken prisoner. Nos 304 and 305 (Polish) Squadrons both formed at Bramcote in November as part of 1 Group, 304 making its first bombing operation on 25–26 April to Rotterdam and continuing on bombing duties until April 1942, transferring to Coastal Command. The squadron flew 488 sorties, dropping some 500 tons of bombs, and lost eighteen aircrew killed or missing. No. 305 (Polish) Squadron started operational flying from Syerston on 25–26 April 1941, remaining with 1 Group until making the last bombing operation on 2–3 August 1943. During 1,117 sorties, 1,555 tons of bombs and mines were dropped, with 136 aircrew killed, ten missing, and thirty-three taken prisoner.

No. 300 (Polish) Squadron formed at Swinderby in August 1940 with Battles, but began re-equipping with Wellington ICs in October. The squadron made 3,684 operational sorties over a period of two and a half years, dropping nearly 10,000 tons of bombs also operating Wellington Mk IVs, Mk IIIs, and B Xs, re-equipping with Lancasters in April 1944.

To provide trained crews for these additional squadrons, the training system expanded with 11 OTU at Bassingbourn and 15 OTU at Harwell starting work in April, followed by 12 OTU at Benson, 18 OTU at Bramcote, and 20 OTU at Lossiemouth by the end of 1940.

Bombing operations began to expand to more distant targets, including Italy with IX Squadron bombing the docks at Venice on 22 December. The first area bombing was authorised against Mannheim on 16 December 1940. Although there were many more bomber squadrons available, the attacks on major German cities and mine-laying were delayed until February 1941 by bad weather, allowing

Wellington B II W5381 PH-C from 12 Squadron being refuelled. (*BAE Systems*)

Wellington B IC LS-S from 15 Squadron. (*BAE Systems*)

Wellington B IC R3295 SR-P from 12 Squadron force-landed on 30 November 1941. (*RAF Museum*)

Wellington W5358 PH-B from 12 Squadron being salvaged after crash landing at Binbrook on 25 July 1941. (*RAF Museum*)

Wellingtons of 300 (Polish) Squadron at Hemswell. (*BAE Systems*)

Wellington B I GR-W from 301 (Polish) Squadron. (*RAF Museum*)

Wellington B IC R1230 NZ-E from 304 (Polish) Squadron. (*RAF Museum*)

Wellington B IC Z1112 NZ-M from 304 (Polish) Squadron. (*RAF Museum*)

Wellington B IC of a Polish squadron being loaded with incendiary bomb canisters in October 1942. (*BAE Systems*)

No. 305 (Polish) Squadron parade.

the established squadrons to regain strength and the new squadrons to become fully operational. The bad weather resulted in many more aborted sorties in addition to navigation difficulties. The replacement as C-in-C Bomber Command of Sir Charles Portal by AM Sir Richard Pierce caused some delays, when the new C-in-C required from the Air Ministry some clarification of the large number of target priorities being requested, continuing the slow-down in Wellington bomber operations for most of the first twelve months of the war.

Despite this slow down, developments of the versatile Wellington continued, probably the most unusual being the directional wireless installation (DWI) to help combat the German magnetic mines. The Vickers Experimental Department at Weybridge was instructed in late 1939 to investigate the possibility of modifying a Wellington fitted with a large de-gausing ring mounted under the airframe, the DWI designation being a method of maintaining security of the project. The de-gausing ring was electrically energised by a 35-kW/310-amp Mawdsley generator driven initially by a 30-hp Ford V8 engine, later replaced by a Gipsy Six Mk II, with a capability of focussing the resulting magnetic field. To make a magnetic mine explode, the Wellington had to be flown over a suspect mine field, triggering a mine without being engulfed itself by the resultant water spout from a successful detonation.

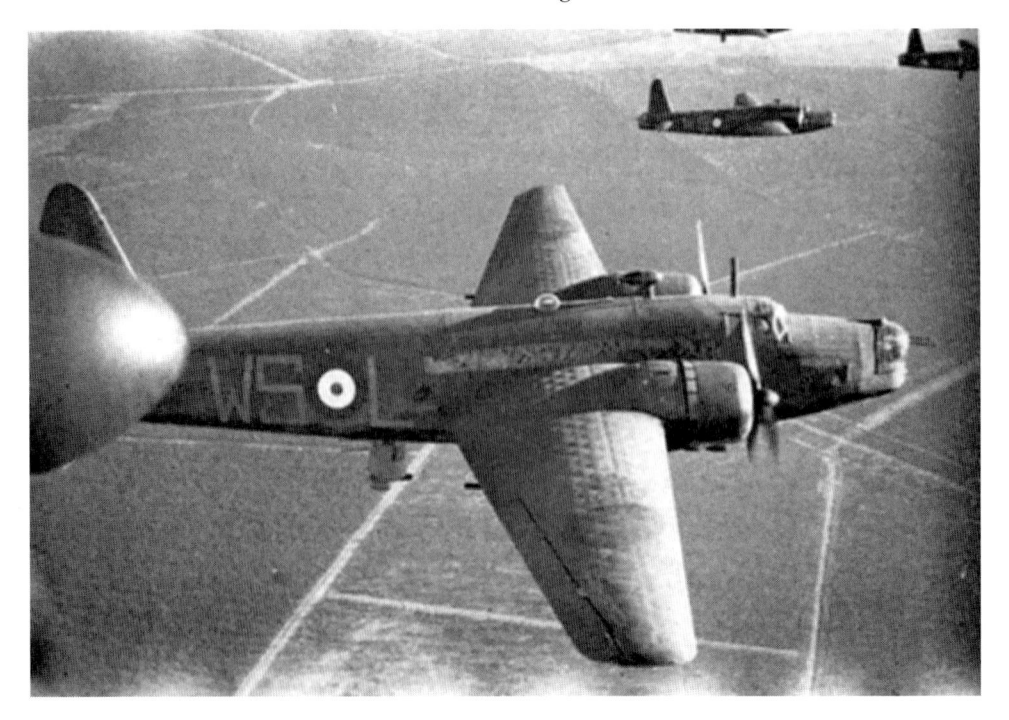

Wellington B IAs from IX Squadron, including WS-L. (*BAE Systems*)

Wellington DW 1 with de-gausing ring on the ground. (*BAE Systems*)

Wellington DW 1 in the air. (*BAE Systems*)

Magnetic mine detonated by Wellington DW 1. (*BAE Systems*)

Wellington DW 1 HX682 with de-gausing ring to remotely detonate magnetic mines. (*BAE Systems*)

The first aircraft to be modified was Mk IA P2518 off the Weybridge production line, with the 48-foot-diameter ring fairing attached. Both front and rear turrets and bomb doors were replaced by streamlined fairings, and the inboard flaps were deleted to avoid downwash from the propellers interfering with the ring aft of the wing trailing edge. Mutt Summers made the first flight on 21 December 1939, and among observers on board was Barnes Wallis. Although the ring had little effect on take-off performance, both acceleration and climb rate were reduced. Following the third test flight, Summers confirmed that stability in roll and pitch were better than the standard aircraft.

No. 1 General Reconnaissance Unit (GRU) was formed at Manston on 19 December 1939 with aircrew detached to 214 Squadron to convert to Wellingtons. The first attempt to set off a mine on the ground at Boscombe Down was on 2 January 1940 by Sqn Ldr Harry Purvis at a height of 50 feet, but without success. Following additional trials at Boscombe Down, the Wellington was flown to Manston to continue trials on 8 January, the first success coming the next day when flying over the Thames Estuary at a surface speed of 170 mph at varying heights. This resulted in success on the seventh run at a height above the surface of 25 to 30 feet. A slight shock was felt in the aircraft, caused by the explosion of the mine. A mine was exploded on the eighth and eleventh test runs at 180 mph, the later causing a considerable shock wave which exceeded 10G, resulting in the tests being halted and the aircraft inspected for damage.

Plans were being made on how to deploy the DWI aircraft effectively in combat operations using a batch of Wellingtons together, keeping the risk of a violent explosion to the minimum. Formation flying at such low level was highly dangerous, and line astern would be hazardous for the following aircraft. A 'vee' formation would endanger the aircraft on the outside of the explosion, and echelon was only possible if the mine was exploded on the side opposite to the formatting aircraft. A shallow 'vee' was adopted for operations with a second Wellington DWI delivered on 15 January 1940 ready for operations to commence in February off Harwich harbour and in the Thames estuary. The first success was on 22 February, although this was a rare event.

Mines were often spotted by naval ships for destruction, but without much success in location by aircraft. Generator problems with the early aircraft resulted in the Ford V8 engine being replaced by the Gipsy Major engine starting with the fifth aircraft, the earlier aircraft being modified. On 4 April the decision was made to convert fifteen Wellingtons, four Mk IAs as DWI Mk Is, and eleven Mk ICs as DWI Mk IIs, with additional conversions made at MUs in the Mediterranean theatre. The first major raid was on 9 May when three Wellingtons escorted by Blenheims of 235 Squadron flew to the Dutch harbour of IJmuiden, which was defended by light flak, commencing the minesweeping run over the harbour approaches and into the harbour, where a Royal Navy destroyer was located. Although no mines were exploded, a channel was kept clear, allowing the Dutch royal family to be evacuated a few days later. It was then decided that DWI Wellingtons could be used more effectively in the Mediterranean with GRU flying its final European sorties on 15 May 1940. The aircraft, apart from one, were ferried to Egypt five days later. The one remaining in Britain P2521, was modified as a message relay aircraft with 138 and 161 Squadron in 1942 at Tempsford to intercept messages from the SOE agents in France and relay them to Britain.

At the start of 1941, although there was a lull in bomber operations, Wellington squadrons were active against German naval shipping and installations. The port of Bremen was the target on 1 January 1941 when more than 100 bombers, including Wellingtons, inflicted significant damage on industrial and residential areas in clear weather, with follow up attacks over the next two nights, causing growing RAF losses to enemy defences. During January, the port of Wilhelmshaven was targeted six times commencing on 8–9 January, when the *Tirpitz* was damaged without loss to the RAF, but on fifth raid on 16–17 January, two Wellingtons failed to return. An attack by twenty-five Wellingtons on the ports of Boulogne and Dunkirk included aircraft from 3 PRU at Oakington to record target damage, with three aircraft being operated from October 1940 to March 1941. During this attack, Wellington L7842 of 311 Squadron made a forced-landing in France with the crew taken prisoner, and the aircraft test flown later by the Luftwaffe.

Bomber Command continued targeting German industrial installations and major cities, together with disrupting oil production. Hanover was targeted on the night of 10–11 February when 112 Wellingtons were part of a bomber force of 222 aircraft, with four Wellingtons lost, although one was shot down over

Norfolk by a night fighter and the crew were able to bail out. The following night, seventy-nine aircraft raided Bremen, but although none were lost to enemy action, eighteen crashed on return to England due to being unable to locate their home bases in bad weather and a lack of fuel. At least the crews were able to abandon the aircraft, although three were killed. Of these aircraft, eight were Wellingtons— one from 99 Squadron, three from 115 Squadron, and two each from 149 and 218 Squadrons.

On 18 February 1941, a 99 Squadron Wellington crew led by Sgt (later Group Captain) J. R. 'Benny' Goodman on a training exercise had the unusual experience of making a claim against a Dornier bomber. While making circuits, there were explosions ahead from Newmarket caused by an enemy bomb attack. Then Goodman looked up to see the Dornier making a gentle turn to the left to assess the results of his bombs. The Wellington came up close below the Dornier without being seen, and both the nose and tail gunners fired, with the enemy aircraft going into the protection of cloud. The Wellington crew were unable to regain contact and returned to base where they reported the incident to the flight commander. Later in the day, the Goodman was recalled by the flight commander who said that a Dornier had crashed some 11 miles from Newmarket and had been claimed by army gunners. Although it could not be confirmed as the Wellington target, it seemed likely and it was declared as half a victory.

No. 405 Squadron was the first of eleven Canadian Wellington units when it formed at Driffield on 23 April 1941 with Merlin-powered Wellington Mk IIs capable of carrying 4,000-lb cookie blast fragmentation bombs. On 8 May 1941, 15 Squadron flew its last Wellington operation, becoming the first to reequip with the 'heavies' when Stirlings arrived at Wyton. That night, Bomber Command sent out a record 364 bombers, with the loss of seven Wellingtons.

Examples of bravery were occurring all the time, some going unrecorded. On 10 May 1941, a 115 Squadron Wellington was part of a raid on Hamburg, which was attacked by a Bf 110 night fighter. The attack knocked out the navigator, Sgt Legg, who recovered consciousness to find the remainder of the crew had abandoned the aircraft. His own parachute was lost through the escape hatch, but he was able to disengage the autopilot and managed to crash land the burning bomber, becoming a POW.

On the night of 7–8 July 1941, an award for supreme gallantry was earned— the Victoria Cross (VC)—by New Zealand-born Sgt James Allen Ward. It was generally believed by all ranks of the British services that for a man to be awarded the VC, he must be either mad or dead. Throughout the Second World War, thirty-two airmen from all services were awarded the VC, of which twenty-three went to bomber crew members. Jimmy Ward was a New Zealander by birth with English parents who had emigrated from Coventry. He grew up in the lush countryside of New Zealand and was fascinated by the Māori traditions and excelled in outdoor sports, including rugby, tennis, and swimming. Young Ward decided on an academic career as a teacher, starting in 1939. With the start of the war, Ward volunteered for the RNZAF, and on 1 July 1940, he was accepted

Wellington Frazer Nash nose gun turret. (*BAE Systems*)

Wellington Frazer Nash tail gun turret. (*BAE Systems*)

Wellington Frazer Nash gun turret interior. (*BAE Systems*)

Wellington flight deck. (*BAE Systems*)

for pilot training. On 29 July 1940, Ward reported for training at 1 EFTS and completed advanced training at 1 SFTS Wigram on 18 January 1941, where he gained his wings and was promotion to sergeant.

Ward set sail for England on 30 January 1941 via Canada, arriving on 6 March, and with fellow Kiwis was posted to 20 OTU at Lossiemouth for conversion to Wellingtons. On completion, he was posted to 75 (NZ) Squadron at Feltwell on 13 June. The next day, his twenty-second birthday he was sent off on his first combat sortie with Düsseldorf as the target. Ward had been crewed with Canadian Sqn Ldr R. P. Widdowson in the left-hand seat, and Jimmy was second pilot. On 7 July, Ward was again second pilot to Widdowson in Wellington L7818 AA-R with Munster as the target, one of ten Wimpies from 75 Squadron, as part of an overall force of forty-nine Wellingtons.

The outbound flight was uneventful with no sign of night fighters or anti-aircraft fire. The crew of L7818 bombed successfully and turned for home. It was a clear moonlit night and then at 13,000 feet over the Netherlands, there was a hail of cannon shells, bullets, and tracers from an enemy night fighter below. The Bf 110 night fighter made hits on the starboard engine, shattering the hydraulic system, causing the bomb doors to drop down creating extra drag. The aircraft communications were also damaged, cutting off the crew. The tail gunner, much to his surprise, saw the belly of the night fighter, and as it banked away for another onslaught, the nineteen-year-old A. J. R. Box fired all four Brownings into the enemy aircraft. The bullets hit at point-blank range; the fighter staggered and fell over on its back, trailing black smoke as it disappeared from view.

No. 75 (NZ) Squadron crews on their way to their aircraft at Stradishall ready for an operation. (*RAF Museum*)

Although badly damaged, the Wimpy flew on, trailing 5-foot flames from ruptured fuel lines feeding the stricken starboard engine, gaining intensity across the fabric-covered wing. Widdowson knew the hazards of the fire rapidly spreading across the fabric, and he turned onto a course flying parallel to the Dutch coast as with only one engine operating and fire spreading rapidly, the captain ordered the crew to prepare for abandonment of the aircraft. As a final comment, the captain said to Ward, 'see if you can put out that bloody fire'.

Ward climbed back through the fuselage, ensuring the crew put on their parachutes, and with the help of two of them began to rip off sections of the fabric above the starboard wing root to see the fire better. Ward let the captain know the fire was still burning, but not getting any worse, so Widdowson, not wishing to be a POW, turned the aircraft towards the North Sea. The captain asked Ward if he could lean out and smother the fire with something, although the flames were still threatening to spread across the fabric. Ward then found stowed canvas cockpit covers, and against the advice of his crew members, he decided to climb out on the wing, restrained by his parachute harness, and tied by a rope around navigator sergeant Lawton's waist.

They removed the 30-inch astrodome to allow Ward to wriggle out into the 100-mph slipstream on to the top of the fuselage, making his way back to the wing, and over 3 feet of its surface to the engine nacelle. Ward kicked hand and toe holes in the fabric, pulling himself slowly towards the burning engine. Ward gripped the canvas cover in his free right hand, stuffing into the flaming hole by the engine, holding it in place until he had to let go due to pain. The slipstream kept trying to break it free, but Ward reached over again and pushed it back in. Seconds later, the wind triumphed and the cover was blown away into the night sky. Ward could see the fire was still there but reduced and prepared to return into the fuselage.

Although by now exhausted, he began the perilous journey back to safety with Lawton holding on to the restraining rope. Ward reached the fuselage and started to climb up to the astrodome aperture, getting his left leg in, but then became stuck with exhaustion. Lawton pulled and managed to get the right leg in and then pulled Ward down into the fuselage where he sat beginning to recover. Once Lawton was sure Ward was improving, he went forward and reported to the captain, who had no idea of what had been going on. The fire was still burning, but not spreading as the fabric had all gone. Widdowson continued on his course towards England. Within 10 miles of the coast, the fire erupted again and suddenly went out. Although the major danger was over, with the damage to hydraulics, there were no flaps and brakes. At 4.30 a.m. on 8 July, the pilot put down on the grass at Newmarket, running the full length of the field before being stopped by the wire boundary fence.

L7818 was repaired, although it did not return to the squadron, and was issued to 15 OTU at Harwell, where it crashed on 8 April 1942 after a mid-air collision with a Spitfire. Ward's squadron commander, Wg Cdr C. E. Kay, following the debrief, made a recommendation for the award for the Victoria Cross which was announced in the *London Gazette* on 5 August 1941. Returning to the squadron, Ward was given his own Wellington and crew to command. On 15 September, he commanded X3205 for an attack against Hamburg; over the target, his aircraft was seen to be illuminated by searchlights, with flak bursts around it. The aircraft fell to earth, burning furiously; the crash killed Jimmy Ward and all but two of his crew.

With the increasing threat of U-boats and FW Condors against Allied shipping, bombing priorities changed in March 1941 to target German aircraft and U-boat bases, as well as factories where they were being built. On the night of 31 March–1 April, six Wellingtons from IX and 149 Squadrons attacked Emden, with an aircraft from each squadron carrying a 4,000-lb 'cookie' blast fragmentation bomb for the first time. To accommodate them, the bomb doors were removed. By this time, the faster Merlin-powered Wellington Mk IIs were replacing the Pegasus-powered Mk ICs. Other U-boat bases bombed included Kiel, Brest, and Lorient, continuing until early July with a reduced perceived threat, allowing other industrial targets to be bombed.

One of the 40 Squadron pilots was Jo Lancaster, who had been an apprentice with Armstrong Whitworth Aircraft at Whitley airfield near Coventry. While

Wellington B IC OJ from 149 Squadron. (*BAE Systems*)

Wellington B II W5437 EP-Q from 104 Squadron at Driffield in September 1941. (*RAF Museum*)

serving his time, he joined the RAF Volunteer Reserve in June 1937, with his basic flying training at Sywell, although he was discharged in 1938. He was called up for the RAF in late 1939 with instructions to report to Cardington as an under-training pilot. In July 1940, he restarted his basic training on Tiger Moths at Desford, moving to 5 FTS and converting to Miles Masters, gaining a recommendation to become a fighter pilot. While at 5 FTS, his flight also received night flying training, which resulted in him being selected for training as a bomber pilot at 20 OTU at Lossiemouth. He was crewed up with a Welshman, a Scotsman, a New Zealander, and two Canadians, completing their work-up on Wellingtons, ready for his first posting to 40 Squadron at Alconbury.

Early operations were fairly relaxed, and Lancaster flew his first eight sorties as second pilot with an experienced captain before being allocated his own Wellington, which was T2701 with the first combat operation to Calais on 9 May 1941. Usually by mid-morning, the crews knew if they were flying on operations that night, and if so, they would fly a night flying test to make sure everything was working. At the briefing, there were no specific routes detailed or specified times of take-off and over target, resulting in each sortie being individual. Each crew had their own ground crew consisting of two engine fitters and two airframe fitters, providing a tightly knit team with pride in their mutual work.

On 24 July 1941, Jo led one of six crews from 40 Squadron in his regular Wellington on a daylight attack against German shipping in Brest Harbour. Flying at 10,000 feet, they made their bombing runs through the barrage of flak and defending Bf 109s. After turning for home, the Wellington was attacked from the rear by a Bf 109, but Jo's rear gunner fired at the fighter, causing the pilot to bail out. During the raid, the Wellington received multiple hits from flak, including a damaged windscreen and a damaged hydraulic system. With a low fuel state, Jo landed safely at St Eval, with no casualties in his crew, unlike some of the other aircraft.

The majority of Jo's bombing missions were at night against targets in the Ruhr and major cities including Berlin, with the longest sortie taking over nine hours to Stettin and back on 29 September, when there was little resistance and the bombs were placed directly on the target. Not all operations were so benign, as on 25 August 1941, just after take-off from Alconbury with full bomb and fuel load, the port engine failed at only 750 feet; Jo fortunately managed to just reach nearby Wyton safely, finding that an oil pipe had broken.

By October 1941, Jo had flown thirty-one sorties with 40 Squadron and was posted on a rest tour to 22 OTU at Wellesbourne Mountford, where as a pilot officer, he became an instructor on Wellingtons, taking part in two of the three 1,000 bomber raids. Jo did not enjoy his duties as an instructor, an example being night flying divided into four three-hour sessions, the 12–3 a.m. and 3–6 a.m. shifts being particularly soul-destroying.

On a day in October 1942, Jo went with a pupil crew on a five-hour cross-country flight, and on returning late afternoon, he found he was detailed to fly a 'Bullseye'. This was a diversionary raid operation by crews under training to draw the attention of German radar early warning systems away from the actual target. Without any food or rest, Jo went off with an entirely novice crew. The wireless operator had his radios in pieces on the aircraft floor, which made the demands of flying around at night worse. Ice was encountered over the Solway Firth, resulting in a decision to abandon the operation and return to base, with flying under cloud being the only way for Jo and his navigator to find their way. He was reprimanded the next day by his chief flying instructor, and as Jo answered back, he was posted back to operations in two days, joining 12 Squadron at Wickenby, making three sorties before the unit converted from Wellingtons to Lancasters. Following his tour with 12 Squadron, Jo was posted to the A&AEE at Boscombe Down on the Armament Testing Squadron where he remained for two years, and in February 1945, he was posted to the Empire Test Pilots' School (ETPS), becoming a test pilot initially with Boulton Paul and then Saunders-Roe where he tested the SRA 1 jet fighter flying boat. He returned to Armstrong Whitworth, flight testing production Lincolns and Meteors, followed by the AW 52 flying wing TS363, from which he had to eject successfully on 30 May 1949, when control was lost due to flutter.

Nuremburg was the target for the first major bombing raid on Germany on 12 October 1941, consisting of 152 aircraft, of which eighty-two were Wellingtons, with seven being lost. With the arrival of Commonwealth crews, four more units were formed, with 401 Squadron at West Raynham in April 1941, followed the same month by 405 (RCAF) Squadron at Pocklington, 458 (RAAF) at Holme-on-Spalding Moor in August, and 460 (RAAF) Squadron at Molesworth in November. Apart from the hazards over the targets, returning bombers had barrage balloons to contend with and enemy night fighters catching the tired crews unexpectedly. A report issued by the vice chief of the Air Staff on 25 May 1941 recorded that in the first twenty days of the month, twenty-five aircraft had been lost or damaged beyond repair and fifty-one were damaged, but repairable, with a further 100 slightly damaged.

The CO of 75 (RNZAF) Squadron at the time was Wg Cdr Percy Pickard, who starred in the RAF propaganda film *Target for Tonight*. Filming was done during the last two weeks of March and the first two weeks of April 1941 with 149 Squadron aircraft as background. Pickard was seconded from 311 (Czech) Squadron to enact the role of captain of a 149 Squadron Wellington P2517 'F' for Freddie. All the cast in the movie were serving RAF personnel.

Percy Charles 'Pick' Pickard joined the RAF in November 1936, commencing pilot training at Perth, moving on to 11 FTS at Wittering where he gained his wings on 22 May 1937. On 4 September, Plt Off. Pickard joined 214 Squadron at Feltwell, flying Handley Page Harrows. With his skills developing both as a pilot and navigator in August 1938, he was appointed as pilot and PA to AVM John Baldwin, AOC Training Command based at Cranwell. Moving on to 7 Squadron on 30 October 1939, he was responsible for the training of operational bomber crews, which later became 16 OTU. After a brief period with 214 Squadron, Pickard joined Wellington-equipped 99 Squadron at Newmarket, participating continually in the bombing programme in the Norwegian and French campaigns.

While flying Wellington N3200 on 19 June against industrial targets in the Ruhr, he was hit by flak in the starboard engine, finally having to ditch in the North Sea, from where the crew were rescued by ASR launch fourteen hours later. By late July 1940, Pickard and his crew had made thirty-one combat sorties and were due for a rest tour, but he and his regular navigator, John 'Bill' Broadley, were seconded to form 311 (Czech) Squadron. With Pickard already promoted to flight lieutenant, he was made acting squadron leader for his new duties. In August 1940, operational training of the Czech crews started with first sorties flown the following month, before the unit moved to East Wretham. Here intensive training continued until the squadron was declared fully operational in December.

By January 1941, Pickard was back on operations, leading the squadron by example over Germany and remaining with the squadron until detached to the Crown Film Unit in March 1941. He had already been awarded the DFC for his tour with 99 Squadron and received the DSO for leading 311 Squadron. On 14 May, he was appointed flight commander of IX Squadron based at Honington,

Wellington B.I AA-N from 75 (NZ) Squadron being prepared for operation. (*RAF Museum*)

Wellington B IC T2835 from 75 (NZ) Squadron. (*BAE Systems*)

again with Wellingtons, returning to operations on 2 June to Düsseldorf, completing eight more sorties in the month. In early August, Pickard's overall operational sorties reached sixty-five in addition to the 'passenger' trips while training the 311 Squadron crews. He was again rested to 3 Group HQ to ferry senior officers around the UK, gaining the rank of wing commander.

On return to combat, Pickard was reunited with Bill Broadley, flying with 161 Squadron at Tempsford on clandestine operations with Allied agents into Europe. By May 1943, Pickard had flown over 100 combat sorties, being promoted to group captain as station commander of RAF Sculthorpe in July 1943. He became leader of Mosquito-equipped 140 Wing, which he led from RAF Hunsdon on the Amiens Prison raid on 18 February 1944, when Pickard and Broadley were shot down and killed by a German Fw 190. Pickard was twenty-eight and Broadley twenty-two.

One of the last Wellington units to be formed in 1941 was 419 RCAF Squadron at Mildenhall on 15 December, receiving its first Mk ICs in January 1942. This was the first of fifteen Wellington squadrons formed that year, and the squadron's initial combat operation was on 11 January, when two aircraft bombed enemy battle cruisers sheltering in the port of Brest. This was also the first of ten Canadian squadrons to receive Wellingtons during the year, but these were balanced out by earlier Wellington squadrons being re-equipped with the heavy four-engined Stirling, Halifax, and Lancaster bombers. In February, 419 Squadron began replacing its earlier Wimpys with Hercules-powered Mk IIIs, which became the main bomber version during 1942 until more of the heavy bombers became available in 1943.

Wellington B IC from 419 Squadron being loaded with a 4,000-lb 'cookie' at Mildenhall on 1 May 1942. (*BAE Systems*)

3
Main Force Operations

On 14 February 1942, Bomber Command was given top priority and was to commence destruction of strategic targets in Germany and manufacturing industry in occupied France. This was issued by the Air Ministry as an area bombing directive. To put this directive into practice, AM Sir Arthur Harris, known as 'Bomber Harris' or 'Butch' to his crews, was appointed AOC Bomber Command to undertake this directive. From his past experience, Harris was aware of the lack of accuracy in hitting targets, poor navigation over long distances, as well as insufficient weight of bombs on targets to achieve the desired destruction. There were often cases of bomber formations being despatched in poor weather with the target not being located or damaged. The new heavy strategic bombers were entering service equipped with H2S ground-mapping radar independent of any external signals. Bombing navigation aid, codenamed GEE was able to indicate the point of release of bombs by two radio beams crossing, providing there was a line of sight for the beams, limiting this navigation aid to shorter ranges. GEE could also be jammed. With new bomber types and aids coming into service, the Wellington force was being reassessed.

Therefore in 1942, Wellington strength in Bomber Command began to slowly decline, although there were a number of new squadrons formed, particularly with Canadian crews. As the year progressed, eighteen RAF squadrons were either deployed to the Mediterranean theatre or re-equipped with Stirlings, Halifaxes, or Lancasters. The first two new squadrons to be equipped with Wellingtons were in February 1942, consisting of 156 Squadron at Alconbury and 158 Squadron at Driffield with Mk IIs. There was then a wait until August when 420 (RCAF) Squadron received Wellingtons at Skipton-on-Swale and 425 (RCAF) Squadron at Dishforth. In October, three units—424 (RCAF) Squadron at Topcliffe, 426 (RCAF) Squadron at Dishforth, and 466 (RAAF) Squadron at Driffield—received Wellingtons. In November, Wellingtons equipped 199 Squadron at Blyton, 427

Croft-based Wellington B III BJ668 ZL-X from 427 Squadron RCAF, November 1943– March 1943. (*BAE Systems*)

Wellington B III X3763 KW-F from 425 (RCAF) Squadron. (*Newark Air Museum*)

(RCAF) Squadron at Croft, 428 (RCAF) Squadron at Dalton, and 429 (RCAF) Squadron at East Moor. The final pair of units in December with Wellingtons was 196 Squadron at Leconfield and 431 (RCAF) Squadron at Burn.

Operations continued to build up during the early part of 1942 in line with the new directive, with large scale pre-planned waves of main force bombers working well. One of these early raids was on the Renault works at Boulogne-Billancourt where heavy road transport was being produced for German land forces. The raid consisted of 235 aircraft, including eighty-nine Wellingtons arriving over the target in three waves. Much to the surprise of the crews, there were no anti-aircraft defences with the loss of only two Wellingtons, a Halifax, and a Stirling, the target being hit accurately. This was the largest number of bombers over a target so far, with a concentration of 121 bombers per hour and the greatest tonnage dropped to date.

The next major raid was 12–13 March on the U-boat works at Kiel, and although bombing was successful, of the sixty-eight Wellingtons despatched, five were lost with all their crews. One other aircraft undershot the runway at Bodney due to engine trouble, but the IX Squadron crew survived without serious injury. Two weeks later on 26–27 March, 104 Wellingtons and eleven Stirlings bombed Essen, but ten Wellingtons were lost due to intense flak; also, it was a clear starlit night to the advantage of night fighters, with four Wellingtons being shot down by the same night fighter in less than fifty minutes. None of the crews from the ten aircraft survived.

Wellington bombing operations were becoming intensive, with minimum breaks between sorties, and defences were strong with anti-aircraft guns guided by searchlights from the ground and very active night fighters. As an example, a typical pace of operations there were ten in a period of twenty-two days, with each one requiring a working day in excess of twelve hours, making the crew very weary, and too exhausted to safely fly. By May 1942, navigation aids were improving in the Wellington fleet with GEE beginning to be fitted.

The build-up led to the Wellington crew's finest hour with the 1,000 bomber raids. The 1,000 bomber raids were Harris's reply to the Nazi's indiscriminate bombing of British cities with their civilian populations. It was not possible, or practical, to send regular 1,000 bomber formations over Germany, but it was a prelude to the Allied bombing campaign. Harris's critics declared bombing would not win the war, but his reply was that it had not been tried yet. It was also the only practical way to take the war to the enemy across occupied Europe, until the invasion could be planned. It was Harris's way of demonstrating to the public in both Britain and Germany, that Bomber Command was now powerful enough to make devastating blows on the German war machine. The plan was approved by the CAS, Sir Charles Portal on 18 May 1942 and approved by PM Churchill two days later.

The overall codename for these operations was Operation Millennium with the first raid on Cologne on 30–31 May, followed by the second on Essen on 1–2 June and the third on Bremen on 25–26 June. The major challenge was to gather

Rolls-Royce Merlin X-powered Wellington B II W5379. (*BAE Systems*)

The 1,590-hp Bristol Hercules-powered Wellington B III BK467. (*BAE Systems*)

together sufficient operational bombers, which was achieved by using crews from the training units, both experienced instructors, and trainees in action for the first time. For the first time, the aircraft were to be in a bomber stream with all aircraft on a common route and speed to and from the target, with each aircraft group allocated a height band to minimise the chance of mid-air collision.

For Codename Trout—the attack on Cologne—a total of 1,047 aircraft were dispatched. No. 1 Group provided 156 Wellingtons; 3 Group, 134 Wellingtons plus eighty-eight Stirlings; 4 Group, nine Wellingtons with 131 Halifaxes and seven Whitleys; 5 Group, 153 aircraft comprising Lancasters, Manchesters, and Hampdens; 91 OTU, 236 Wellingtons plus twenty-one Whitleys; 92 OTU, sixty-three Wellingtons plus forty-five Hampdens, and four more Wellingtons from Training Command. With 602 Wellingtons deployed, it was well over half the total force, and never before had so many Wellingtons gone into action. All the squadrons were represented with 12 Squadron despatching twenty-eight Mk IIs and ninety-two OTU, which sent thirty-five aircraft. As a result, 868 bombers attacked Cologne, causing considerable damage and a number of industrial targets destroyed. Total RAF bomber losses were fifty-three aircraft, including thirty-four Wellingtons. Most of the losses were due to night fighters, as ground defences were spasmodic with little search-light activity.

As part of the overall force, 15 OTU despatched twenty Wellingtons from Harwell, with another ten from the satellite at Hampstead Norris, twenty-three reaching the target and achieving good results, while two aircraft failed to return, some of the trainees going on their first combat sortie. With flying training suspended towards the end of May, the instructors were told to form crews up including trainees, although some of the OTU Wellingtons were becoming worn out and sluggish in performance. Some of the OTU aircraft were positioned for the raid nearer the front line, as normally, training stations were in the quieter western part of Britain, an example being 26 OTU crews deployed to Graveley on 27 May, which had only just completed construction. Crews were accommodated in spartan conditions without any knowledge of why they were there. The next day at briefing, the target was revealed to the crews, and they would be taking part in a momentous 1,000 bomber raid, the single target being Cologne.

With a very short break, while the bombers were redeployed, the second 1,000 bomber raid was on Essen on the night of 1 June with the Codename Stoat. The principal aiming point at Essen was the major Krupps industrial complex, and the final total of aircraft available was 956, including 545 Wellingtons. The leaders were twenty-four pathfinding Wellingtons from Feltwell, Honington, Marham, and Oakington, carrying illuminating flares, dropped from zero hour to zero plus twenty-three minutes, with the first wave of bombers to release their loads at zero hour plus two minutes. Due to the weather being poorer than on the Cologne raid, bombing was scattered, with fifteen Wellingtons failed to return out of a total of thirty-one bombers lost. The OTU crews suffered higher losses with five aircraft destroyed by night fighters.

Both 1,000 bomber raids had caused considerable disruption to the training programme due to the involvement of the OTUs, but a third was made with Operation Salmon, an attack on Bremen taking place during the night of 25–26 June 1942. The force despatched was again just short of 1,000 bombers, with a total of 960 aircraft, of which 472 were Wellingtons. The target for 5 Group was the Focke-Wulf factory, while the remainder of the bombers bombed the docks and city, but cloud cover reduced accuracy. A total of 696 bombers claimed to have reached the target, causing considerable damage, but unfortunately, forty-eight aircraft failed to return with the highest total from OTU aircraft with twenty-one lost, nine to night fighters.

The three 1,000 bomber raids launched Harris's strategic bombing offensive on the Third Reich, with major raids on industry, ship production, and harbours, as well as including mine-laying. With improved accuracy following marking during the 1,000 bomber raids, it was clear that an elite force needed to be formed to maintain a higher level of accuracy. The Pathfinder Force (PFF) was formed in August 1942 under the command of Air Cdr Donald Bennett, later becoming 8 Group. With the increased sophistication of German defences, the Wellington force began to suffer increased losses due to the poor performance of the aircraft. Examples were on a Duisburg raid on 21–22 July; ten Wellingtons failed to return out of 170 despatched. Less than a week later, fifteen out of 181 were lost during an attack on Hamburg. Not only were these loss rates becoming unsustainable, but they were higher than the more modern bombers being introduced into operation. Therefore, the priority was to re-equip the Bomber Command Wellington squadrons with the new types entering service and to provide enough aircraft to equip bomber squadrons in overseas theatres where the risks were not so great.

Meanwhile, a 142 Squadron crew were tasked for a mine-laying sortie on the approaches to Brest harbour on 7 November 1942. After leaving over Portland Bill the radio receiver was unserviceable, but the crew decided to continue to the target with the radio unserviceable, even though they should have abandoned the sortie. The aircraft descended to dropping height over the sea, and with the engine power reduced, the mines were released in the harbour approaches. Opening up the engines in a tight turn to port, there was a violent explosion in the rear fuselage from ground fire. Despite the damage, a course was set for home, climbing to 4,000 feet. On inspection, there was a large hole in the aircraft underside, causing a freezing gale through the aircraft, with the rear gunner brought forward ahead of the damage. As they returned over southern England, the weather became worse with thick cloud and rain, descending to 2,000 feet in the cloud. A call was made to base at Waltham where a safe landing was made after a flight of seven hours and forty-five minutes to discover that the raid had been aborted, which the crew had not received due to failed radio. The crew had been the only ones flying that night in 1 Group and were reprimanded as they should have aborted when the radio went u/s. They later had the satisfaction of learning an enemy freighter had been blown up by a mine on approach to Brest, which was claimed unofficially by the crew.

Doug Newham was an air observer (navigation and bomb aiming) with 150 Squadron at Kirmington, where he was posted from 156 Squadron on 6 November 1942. No. 156 Squadron in 1 Group based at Warboys had GEE fitted to its Wellington B IIIs and specialised in target marking prior to the Pathfinder Force being established. Doug's first combat operation was a 'gardening' sortie to La Rochelle, followed by a similar mine-laying trip to Lorrent four nights later. Doug's first and only bombing operation from Britain with his regular pilot—Sgt Harris—and crew was to Stuttgart on 22 November 1942. A small detachment from the squadron then departed on 9 December for Algeria via Gibraltar.

Doug Newham had started his navigation training at 2 AOS Millom on 8 December 1941, which was equipped with the totally ineffective Bothas. He only made three sorties in these aircraft before they were withdrawn and Doug went to No. 1 Elementary Air Observers School at Eastbourne for ground school navigation training, while awaiting a posting to an air observers school (AOS). Doug moved to No. 5 AOS at Jurby on the Isle of Man on 12 January 1942 for further practical flying training, flying in Ansons. A conversion was made to Blenheims on 9 February, where he trained as a navigator/air gunner, and also flew in Hampdens as a bomb aimer. The course was completed on 26 June when he was promoted from leading aircraftman to sergeant. This was followed by a posting to 19 OTU at Kinloss from 25 July for more advanced navigation training in Ansons and Whitleys until 2 September, ready for his posting to 156 Squadron where he joined with a regular crew.

By the end of 1942, Halifaxes had replaced Wellingtons with 103, 158, 405, and 460 (RAAF) Squadrons; Lancasters with IX, 12, 57, and 101 Squadrons; and Stirlings with 75, 214, and 218 Squadrons. Meanwhile, 40 and 150 Squadrons had moved to the Mediterranean and 99 and 215 had gone to India. Due to the increased Atlantic U-boat threat, Harris reluctantly agreed to release 304 and 311 (Polish) Squadrons and 458 (RAAF) Squadrons to Coastal Command. During this run-down, on 1 May 1943, 432 (RCAF) Squadron formed at Skipton-on-Swale with Wellington Mk Xs, but in October, they were replaced by Lancasters at East Moor. Another late unit to be equipped with Wellingtons was 466 (RAAF) Squadron with Mk IIs at Driffield on 15 October 1942, replacing them a month later by Mk Xs and moving to Leconfield on 22 December, where it equipped with Halifaxes in September 1943.

Probably the most disastrous Wellington raid was the bombing of Nuremberg on 28–29 August, when the force was 159 aircraft, of which forty-one were Wellingtons, with fourteen failing to return to base, making an unsustainable loss rate of 34 per cent. Five came from 115 Squadron, although fortunately, not all the crews were killed.

With the build-up of Bomber Command's heavy bomber force, ready for a sustained assault on German industry, communications, and oil resources at the beginning of 1943, there were still nineteen Wellington squadrons in the order of battle. The last to form was 166 Squadron at Kirmington on 27 January from

Wellington B IC R1459 PM-X from 103 Squadron at Elsham Wolds on 23 October 1941 after a forced-landing. (*RAF Museum*)

elements of 142 and 150 Squadrons. The squadron operated Mk IIIs until April, with Mk Xs arriving from February, and the squadron re-equipped with Lancasters in September of the same year. On 13 February, 166 Squadron despatched fourteen Wimpys among a force of 377 bombers, including ninety-nine Wellingtons against Lorient. All 166 Squadron's aircraft bombed successfully and turned for home.

Having safely crossed the English coast at 8,000 feet, BK460 flown by FS George Ashplant was struck from below by a 158 Squadron Halifax. One of the crew was killed in the impact as the underside of the aircraft nose was destroyed and both engines were torn from their mountings. Ashplant ordered the crew to abandon the aircraft, but the bomb aimer's parachute had fallen out in the collision, and the captain gave him his. Using great skill, Ashplant managed to make a successful crash landing, resulting in the first award to a Wellington crew of the Conspicuous Gallantry Medal (CGM), which ranked only second to the VC. Sadly, this brave man was lost on 24 July during the first of the great firestorm raids on Hamburg.

Harris's 'Battle of the Ruhr' commenced in March 1943 and continued until the end of July. It was intended to be an all-out effort to destroy Germany's manufacturing industry around the extensive coalfields; the high pollution caused some difficulty with locating targets due to poor visibility. Following this, in

May 1943, was the most significant event in Bomber Command strategy, with the USAAF 8th Air Force joining the bombing of enemy targets. While Bomber Command continued with night bombing, the US 8th AF bombed during daylight, keeping on the pressure round the clock against industrial targets. By this time, Bomber Command was able to field 600 bombers a night, rising to 800 from July, and as the PFF became established, the accuracy improved significantly. By this stage, the Wellington force was operating at reduced numbers, with some operations not using the type at all.

Halifaxes replaced Wellingtons with 425, 427, 428, 429, and 431 (RCAF) and 466 (RAAF) Squadrons; Lancasters re-equipped 156, 426 (RCAF) and 432 (RCAF); 196 and 199 Squadrons received Stirlings; and 305 (Polish) Squadron had a change of role and flew Mitchells. No. 420 (RCAF) Squadron moved to the Mediterranean in May, and 301 (Polish) Squadron disbanded at Hemswell on 7 April. As the Wellington part of the main force reduced, crews were still sent to targets in the Ruhr, Wuppertal being one of the more effective on 29–30 May. Wellington crews were also included on raids to Düsseldorf, Mulheim, Krefeld, Gelsenkirchen, and Aachen, leading up to the Battle of Hamburg, which commenced on 27–28 July, when there were only seventy-four Wellingtons out of 787 bombers overall, and only one was lost.

A typical day in Bomber Command operations during the Second World War was started with the ground crew up early in the morning, preparing their aircraft, many of which could have been damaged by enemy action. The ground crew team consisted of fitters, riggers, and armourers, plus other specialists. The aircraft that were serviceable had their daily inspection (DI) and any defects reported from the last flight corrected, mostly with the aircraft dispersed around the airfield in all weathers.

All the aircraft systems were checked and any combat damage repaired. The controls were checked to ensure free movement, and hydraulics and pneumatics were checked for any leaks or malfunction. Brakes and tyres were checked, as were radio functions and aircraft lights. Engine ground runs were made to check for magneto 'mag' drops, fuel or oil leaks, power checks, plus temperatures and unwanted vibration. The aircraft was refuelled and once declared serviceable and the form 700 signed, the aircrew would take it up on a short night-flying test, following which any snags were cured and the fuel and oil topped up. Preparations could then start for operations that night, arming the guns. There was a great pride in keeping the aircraft in the best possible operational capability whatever the condition, the ground crew only loaning it to the air crew with orders to bring it back safely.

By lunchtime, targets would have been identified and signals sent to the stations by teleprinters with the operational order, which was received by the station senior staff, and preparations were made for air crew briefing. Sometimes there was more than one target, with some designated as diversions to mask the primary target in the hope of confusing the night fighter defences. On the night of 30 August, 33 OTU Wellingtons were allocated, the first time since the 1,000 bomber raids

Wellington B II T2545. (*BAE Systems*)

Wellington B III BK563 on a rather damp apron. (*BAE Systems*)

that crews under training were deployed in combat. They shared the raid with Halifaxes and Obeo-equipped Mosquitos. The main force included fifty-seven Wellingtons with Lancasters, Halifaxes, Stirlings and Mosquitos with targets at Monchengladbach and Reydt, while the OTU Wellingtons were allocated ammunition storage depot at the Forest of Éperlecques in Northern France. Both forces were to be ready at 10 p.m. for a departure at midnight.

Once the number of serviceable aircraft was known, lists were put up in the various messes designating the crews detailed to fly that night, with a call to briefing during the late afternoon. This was when the target was revealed for the first time, and details were given for take-off time, time over target, and weather to be expected to, over, and on the return from the target. Anticipated defences were briefed and routes designated to avoid known hotspots of anti-aircraft defences. Altitude separation was provided to avoid confliction in the target area, and instructions to aim for relevant colour target indicators (TI). Following the overall briefing, there were then specialist briefings for navigators, as well as other crew members, after which the crews got together to discuss the sortie. The crews then returned to their respective messes for a night time flying supper.

With the target identified, the ground crew could prepare the aircraft with its bomb load with weight and range required, and the calculations made for the fuel required, which could be fairly demanding. The Wellington Mk III, for example, was fitted with three wing tanks forward holding 150 gallons and three tanks aft containing 167 gallons in both wings. Each engine nacelle contained a 58-gallon fuel tank, and various overload tanks could be fitted with a capacity of up to another 185 gallons, which could be located in the bomb bay when ferrying the aircraft over extended ranges. Bombs were delivered to the aircraft on special trolleys from the bomb store and were hand-winched into the aircraft by an integral winch, each bomb having its fuse set for correct timing. The detonator and fins were attached and a safety wire attached to the bomb carrier. The final load distribution was then passed to the bomb aimer, who set up the bomb panel in the aircraft nose. The bomb load could vary between squadrons to obtain the greatest destructive effect.

With the aircraft ready for departure, the ground crew 'chiefy', or senior NCO, would control the engine starting in communication with the pilot. Each engine was primed by an airman, and the mobile battery trolley (trolley acc) disconnected after providing the power to start the engines. The aircraft were then ready to taxi to the runway threshold, and given clearance to take-off by an Aldis lamp in the runway caravan, maintaining strict radio silence to avoid alerting the enemy of an impending raid. It was not just enemy defences which were hazardous, as two 466 (RAAF) Wellingtons collided on 30 August 1943 over the town of Goole after take-off from Leconfield, one aircraft falling on the centre of the town with three people killed on the ground in addition to the ten crew members of the two aircraft.

The main force arrived over the target in good weather conditions, to find it accurately marked by Oboe Pathfinder Mosquitos, with each bomb aimer setting the wind speed and direction into his bomb sight as the aircraft approached the target, indicating to the pilot that it was ready to bomb, who then fused the bombs ready for release. This was the point where the aircraft was at greatest risk, with the bomb aimer instructing the pilot to correct any drift. On entering the danger area, the pilot selected the bombs until the bomb aimer released them when the sight coincided with the target and confirming the number of bombs released. The pilot continued to fly the straight and level at a steady altitude until the bomb aimer reported 'bombs plotted', allowing the target photograph to be taken using the fixed vertically mounted F24 camera. Once this had been achieved, the tension was released as the pilot turned the aircraft away from the target and the navigator set the course for home.

If any bombs were not released over the target, there were specific instructions, with jettisoning only if unavoidable, the bombs having been made safe first. Alternatively, if there were bombs being carried on the return to base, they were to be made safe as soon as the decision was made, and on arrival back home, the bomb doors were only to be opened by a qualified armament officer.

As the surviving aircraft returned to base, the ground crew would be waiting to welcome them, but sadness from those whose crew failed to return. Four Wellingtons and crews were lost on the Monchengladbach and Reydt raid out of a total loss of thirty bombers. The returning aircraft were then inspected for any damage requiring repairing before the next operation, the weary aircrew making their way for a debriefing with the intelligence officers prior to being fed a hot supper and going to bed. The next morning, a signal had arrived from the AOC, congratulating the crews on excellent results achieved with accurate hits on the TIs.

By early October 1943, Wellingtons were almost withdrawn from combat in Bomber Command. On the night of 7–8 October, Wellington Mk X HF490 of 300 Squadron was the last of the type in Bomber Command to be lost to enemy action. The crew were tasked with a 'gardening' operation to St Nazaire in poor weather. The aircraft took off from Ingham and never returned with its Polish crew of five. The final Wellington participation in a Bomber Command raid was on the night of 8–9 October during an attack on Hanover, when twenty-six of the type from 300 and 432 Squadrons joined Lancasters, Halifaxes, and Mosquitos. Despite all Wellingtons returning after the raid, twenty-seven other bombers were lost. After this raid, Wellingtons provided support for bomber raids in specialist roles within 100 Group. The Wellingtons had completed four years and one month of combat—a record for any RAF medium or heavy bomber, the closest rival being the Stirling with three years and seven months of active service.

Bomber Command relied heavily on a number of second line support units, many equipped with Wellingtons. The Central Gunnery School at Sutton Bridge, although mainly for fighter pilots' gunnery training, also had a flight of Wellingtons used for training gunnery leaders with bomber squadrons, often bringing the fighter and bomber crews together during exercises. Other more mundane, but essential tasks were target towing for gunnery training, ferry training for delivery of operational aircraft to new bases, and training foreign aircrews in the use of English.

New systems development used Wellingtons for flight and operational trials, which could take them into harm's way. The wireless intelligence unit at Boscombe Down was redesignated 109 Squadron in December 1940 with the tasks of developing radar aids and identifying German radio beams used to assist in enemy bomber navigation to targets in Britain. These had first been located in June 1940. In July 1942, the squadron split into two special duties flights, with 1473 Flight at Upper Heyford specialising in radio countermeasures, while 1474 Flight at Stradishall was mainly concerned with enemy radar wavelength detection. With a fleet of four to five Wellingtons, the duties included window trials for radar spoofing and homing flights. They also specialised in identifying and detecting radio beams which directed enemy bombers to their targets. Wideband receivers were fitted to interrogate enemy early warning radars. These operations were known as 'ferrets'.

On the night of 2–3 December 1942, a Wellington from 1474 Flight was acting as bait in the Frankfurt area, investigating enemy AI radar; the intention was to attract the attention of an enemy night fighter to identify the radar and radio frequencies being used. The Wellington was subject to an attack by a Ju 88 night fighter, wounding the special operator who had picked up the transmissions. Despite being severely wounded during the attack, he was able to identify the night fighter's radar frequencies, providing excellent intelligence on the new Lichtenstein radar. Following up to twelve attacks, the Ju 88 broke off by which time the aircraft was down to 500 feet. Fortunately, the pilot was able to get back to England, ditching in the sea close to the Kent coast at Deal.

In April 1943, 1473 Flight started 'Jostle' jammer trials, which was first used to jam German tank communications in North Africa. It was further developed for use by 100 Group to disrupt German radar and night fighter communications. The two flights were merged into 192 Squadron on 4 January 1943 at Gransden Lodge with a mix of Wellington IC, II, and X on specialist highly classified signals work.

The operator's duties were to locate radio beams being transmitted from Holland and France and track them, giving some indication of the target for that night. Other duties included joining the incoming German bomber formations to check the effectiveness of the ground jamming, the intention being to ensure beam guidance ceased well out from the English coast.

Another countermeasures unit was the Fighter Interception Development Squadron (FIDS) based at Ford in Sussex, equipped with a variety of aircraft. In late 1944, when the ground-launched V1 sites were being overrun by the Allies, Germany began to air launch V1s from He 111s. To counter this threat, FIDS planned to operate an ASV (air-to-surface vessel) radar-equipped Wellington patrolling off the Dutch coast at around 4,000 feet to detect the launch aircraft approaching Britain. When one was detected, an accompanying Mosquito fighter was guided to intercept. When tried for the first time on 13 January 1945, a slow-moving target was detected on the radar, but when the Mosquito approached to intercept, the aircraft was another Wellington. No further attempts were made by the Luftwaffe to air launch the V1s, resulting in the FIDS programme being abandoned.

Operational requirement OR.94 was issued in 1938 by the Air Ministry for a bomber capable of operating at a cruising height of 35,000 feet with an endurance of 2,200 miles. Vickers proposed adapted Wellington airframes as the Mk V and Mk VI versions, with Specifications B.23/39 and B.17/40 written around them. The major change was the installation of a prominent pressure cabin in the forward fuselage and a 12-foot increase in wingspan. There was very little experience of pressure cabins at the time, resulting in the Vickers design team working from basic principles. With technical success on the project, the company would gain useful pioneering experience in the concept as a bomber operating at high altitude would not only be above the ground-based anti-aircraft guns, but also less vulnerable to fighters.

The main difference between the two versions was the Mk V was powered by a pair of Hercules Mk VIII engines and the Mk VI with supercharged Merlin 60s. As the Hercules engines were incapable of providing sufficient power to attain the desired ceiling, development concentrated on the 1,600-hp two-stage Merlin 60. Prototypes were constructed at the Vickers Experimental Department at Foxwarren near Cobham, making first flight of Mk V R3298 on 25 September 1940 to the less vulnerable airfield at Squires Gate. Testing commenced at Boscombe Down with W5795, but on 12 July 1942, the aircraft dived at high speed from altitude, breaking up on the way down and killing the crew. The most likely cause was the failure of a propeller blade, which penetrated the pressure cabin and disabled the pilot.

The first Mk VI W5796 made its initial flight in November 1941 and was capable of reaching the specified altitude of 40,000 feet. As a demonstration of its performance Mk VI DR484 was taken to 34,000 feet, which took fifty minutes to achieve, and flew a range of 1,100 miles, the height over the target being 37,100 feet. The crew of four were all housed in the pressure cabin, consisting of a pilot, navigator, bomb aimer, and radio operator. There were no gunners required as the turrets were operated remotely from the cabin and sighted by a periscope. The intention was for the Mk VI to operate as a pathfinder aircraft with Bomber Command, and was evaluated by one flight of 109 Squadron at Stradishall between March and July 1942. They were allocated four aircraft as GEE trainers and for Oboe trials with the Telecommunications Flying Unit (TFU) at Defford.

Deliberations by the Air Staff questioning the value of high-altitude bombers resulted in only a short production batch of sixty-four Mk VIs. The last was delivered in January 1943 but was struck off charge (SOC) by March. The last to fly was Mk VI W5802, which was used by Rotol for trials before being SOC on 11 November 1945. The remainder of the production run was withdrawn and scrapped between March 1943 and August 1944.

Wellington B V R3298 being assembled at Brooklands with the pressure cabin fitted. (*BAE Systems*)

Close-up of pressure cabin in Wellington B V at Brooklands. (*BAE Systems*)

Front view of Wellington B V with pressure cabin assembly at Brooklands awaiting installation of engines. (*BAE Systems*)

Complete Wellington B V powered by a pair of 1,425-hp Hercules engines at Brooklands. (*BAE Systems*)

Wellington B V R3298 was first flown from Brooklands on 25 September 1940. (*BAE Systems*)

Wellington B V prototype R3298. (*BAE Systems*)

Wellington B VI close-up of front end showing the pressure cabin and Rolls-Royce Merlin power. (*BAE Systems*)

The starboard Rolls-Royce Merlin installation on Wellington B VI. (*BAE Systems*)

Wellington B VI W5796. (*BAE Systems*)

Wellington B VI W5796. (*BAE Systems*)

Wellington B VI W5798. This aircraft was the first of a batch of twenty-seven Mk Vs re-engined with Merlins. It served with RAE and A&AEE on Sperry gyro bomb site development. (*BAE Systems*)

Wellington B VIG DR484. (*BAE Systems*)

4
Aircrew Training

Initially, Wellington crew training was the responsibility of the early squadrons, but as the force increased, a massive training programme was created at operational training units (OTUs), which were mostly located in the west and north of Britain, away as much as possible from Luftwaffe attention. Each member of the aircrew would have received his basic and specialist training before arriving at the OTU, and this is where the crews formed themselves together in the informal way of being put into a room and left to their own devices. In most cases, this worked well and created a bond between the various specialist crew skills to the mutual benefit of the whole.

The first batch of seven OTUs were formed on 8 April 1940 with the task of training night bomber crews for Bomber Command, in many cases equipped with earlier types such as Whitleys. No. 10 OTU was formed at Abingdon in 6 Group with the first Wellingtons arriving in June 1940, and a strength of forty aircraft by August, the last Whitley departing the following month. There were satellite airfields allocated at Stanton Harcourt and Mount Farm to spread the training programme. By 2 December, the OTU was up to full strength with fifty-four Wellingtons, including a Polish flight, and example being Mk X HE580 ZG-V. The unit disbanded on 10 September 1946.

No. 11 OTU was formed at Bassingbourn in 6 Group from 215 Squadron with fifty-two Wellingtons and a satellite at Steeple Morden. Steeple Morden was opened in an incomplete state on 8 April 1940 and housed B and D Flights, while Bassingbourn accommodated A, C, and E Flights. The two airfields had a total of over 100 aircraft including Ansons used for navigation and radio training. By May 1940, there were fifty-four Wellingtons on the strength in addition to Ansons. Bassingbourn was an RAF Expansion Scheme permanent airfield, while Steeple Morden was rapidly created for the needs of war, featuring very few permanent structures. Evidence of this is that Bassingbourn still exists as a military base, while Steeple Morden has returned to agriculture.

The instructors, who were on a 'rest' tour from operations, found aircrew training more hazardous than operations. Many of them had not been on an instructor's course, and the trainee pilots had only experience of Tiger Moths, Harvards, and Oxfords, making conversion to the 10-ton, twin 1,050-hp engines and over 86-foot-wingspan Wellington somewhat daunting. As a start, the trainee pilots would do a few take-offs and landings with the instructor flying the Wimpy, followed by more take-offs and landings from the left-hand seat, with the instructor alongside. When they had proved their competence, they were sent solo and continued to hone their skills with more circuits and bumps, initially in daylight, but then at night. Ground training included lectures in engine handling, bombing theory, dinghy drill, meteorology, and fighter evasion.

Air observers were responsible for navigation and bomb aiming and in general started at the OCU with only thirty hours of solo navigation, all in daylight. Once experiencing night navigation in blackout conditions, the observer could easily become lost, often relying on other members of the crew to help with identifying landmarks. The final training for the wireless/air gunner crew members started in classroom cubicles, simulating aircraft installations, followed by flying experience in Ansons, taking turns to practice air-to-ground transmissions.

Air gunner training consisted of air firing at target drogues towed by Bassingbourn-based Lysanders, and also ground-based targets, with ground-based training firing machine guns on the butts. To give some idea of the intensity of training, the operations record book for July 1942, gunners fired 148,700 rounds on air-to-air targets, 7,600 rounds at ground targets and 400 rounds on operations. The Wellington ICs used by the OCU were armed with two 0.303-inch machine gun turrets in the nose and tail, with two beam-mounted 0.303-inch machine guns. The crews consisted of a pilot, navigator, bomb aimer, wireless operator/air gunner, and rear gunner, mostly being newly qualified sergeants.

In the early days, there were many accidents with twenty Wellingtons being destroyed in as many days at Bassingbourn, often caused by inadvertently landing with the wheels still retracted despite the warning claxon sounding in the cockpit. The wheels-up landings were often reparable due to the strong structure of the aircraft, which could take much of the shocks of student mishandling. With training continuing round the clock, many of the aircraft were flying up to eighteen hours every twenty-four, with servicing carried out in the open in all weathers. The ground crews worked a weekly rota with a change over from days to nights every Friday, the changeover period for night work being twenty-four hours from 8 a.m. Friday to 8 a.m. Saturday. The following Friday, they had twenty-four hours off. Many of the aircraft were tired veterans of combat, and maintaining them in flying condition was a challenge, particularly in the open.

Once local flying had been mastered, training moved on to long-distance cross-country night flights with more opportunities for accidents. As many as 25 per cent were lost before completing their courses with 5,327 officers and men killed and a further 3,113 injured in Bomber Command training, the most likely

A not uncommon occurrence at an OTU—a belly-landed Wellington being defueled ready for salvage and possible repair. (*BAE Systems*)

cause being inexperience and the extremely short period of training in the early stages of the war.

In September 1940 at Bassingbourn, two Wellingtons were fitted with large tanks in the bomb bays to be filled with petrol for spreading by pipes over the invasion beaches and ignited by the rear gunner firing incendiary bullets—an improvisation fortunately never used.

Both Bassingbourn and Steeple Morden were targets for enemy bombs, and by 31 March 1941, 11 OTU completed training of fifteen pilots, five observers, and two wireless operators/air gunners. During this period, 1,429 hours were flown in daylight and 417 hours at night. On 10 April at night, Steeple Morden was the target for ten high-explosive bombs, only one of which exploded; just after midnight, another eight bombs were dropped with incendiaries, resulting in a temporary stop to night flying. Also on 10 April, Wellington I L4253 was shot down by an unidentified raider during its final circuit and crashed near Ashwell station, but fortunately, both pilot and pupil escaped without injury. On 18 April at 2.25 a.m., Mk I L4302 stalled while on circuit training at Steeple Morden and crashed at Abington Piggotts, killing both crew members, bringing a total of twenty-nine crew members killed or missing at 11 OTU since 1940.

On 7 May, Wellington N3227 was on approach to land at Steeple Morden when it was attacked at 900 feet by a Ju 88. The rear gunner responded to the enemy fire, but by then, the port wing fuel tank was on fire and the pilot made a forced-landing at Wendy, with all three crew members escaping with minor injuries. A complete crew of seven was lost on 9 June when R1728 took off on a navigation exercise from Steeple Morden over the North Sea, and nothing further was heard. During June, a total of 1,892 day flying training hours were achieved with another 1,158 hours of night flying from both Bassingbourn and Steeple Morden.

A serious loss was on 22 July when Wellington R1334 was being flown by Sgt F. S. Housten at 1.30 a.m. in light rain. The aircraft was circling, waiting its turn to land at Steeple Morden with three pilots, four wireless operators, and an observer on board. While at 600 feet close to Ashwell church, they were attacked by a Ju 88 night fighter, which collided with the Wellington. Both aircraft fell in balls of fire, killing all on board the aircraft; the wreckage fell on the edge of the village. The pilot of the Ju 88 was *Leutnant* Heinz Volker with previous seven claims, the Wellington being his posthumous eighth. On 13 August, Bassingbourn was the target with four high-explosive bombs dropped with incendiaries, hitting a barrack block, killing ten and injuring a further twelve airmen.

By August, the total of aircraft on 11 OTU strength was fifty-four Wellingtons, eighteen Ansons, and two Lysanders with twenty-seven Wellington crews trained. In September, sixty-one pilots, thirty-one observers, sixty-four wireless operators/air gunners, and twenty-five air gunners completed their training with a total of 2,314 flying hours.

When ACM Sir Arthur Harris became C-in-C Bomber Command in early May 1942 his plan for 1,000 bomber raid on Germany was approved by Winston Churchill. The aim was to destroy a city in one night, and Hamburg was chosen with Cologne as the alternative. The operation was to be mounted in a full moon period in the last week of May. This operation was to include all RAF bombing units, including OTUs, and when news of the operation reached Bassingbourn, all air crews on leave returned immediately and all leave was cancelled. No. 11 OTU was to supply twelve Wellingtons and crews from Bassingbourn and a further thirteen from Steeple Morden. Preparations included around-the-clock maintenance to ensure the aircraft were fully airworthy. With poor weather delaying the start, Harris decided that Cologne would be the target, and on 31 May, 1,046 bombers were despatched. Instructors were mostly flying or navigating the bombers, with trainees as the rest of the crew, facing combat for the first time.

While crossing the Dutch coast, the weather was clear and Cologne was clearly visible. There was moderate to heavy flak in the target area, and only one aircraft was lost from 11 OTU. Some 890 crews claimed to have bombed the target, but forty aircraft overall failed to return. Harris targeted Essen on 1 June, and 11 OTU sent twenty Wellingtons, although the raid was not a total success due to cloud cover and haze. However, 956 bombers took off, with 767 claiming to have hit the target, and one 11 OTU Wellington failed to return to Steeple Morden. With much relief after two nights on operations, the OTUs were instructed to revert to training, but on 25 June, Harris ordered a third 1,000 bomber raid.

This 1,000 bomber raid was on Bremen, and 11 OTU supplied twenty-five Wellingtons towards a total force of 1,006 RAF bombers. Eleven 11 OTU bombers attacked the target, bombing through cloud cover, for the loss of three Steeple Morden-based aircraft, and although the raid was considered an overall success, it was not as much as Cologne. By the end of June, 11 OTU had flown 2,093 training hours during the month on Wellingtons and Ansons.

On 31 July, the 11 OTU HQ at Bassingbourn received an order that they were to participate in Operation Grand National, which was an attack on Düsseldorf. A total of eighteen aircraft from both Bassingbourn and Steeple Morden were allocated to the raid, with twelve Wellingtons successfully bombing the target, resulting in widespread fires. The other six aircraft had to return with engine trouble before reaching the target, underlining the worn-out state of the bombers, particularly the engines.

Training accidents continued with DV718 during the night of 1–2 September while flying a cross-country navigation exercise; it hit high ground in bad weather, colliding with the Pennines, killing all but one of the crew, the surviving navigator being severely injured. Another 11 OTU Wellington, Z8808, on the same night hit high ground in the Yorkshire Dales in a forced-landing caused by control difficulties. Fortunately, the aircraft did not catch fire, and although the crew were injured, they survived. Both aircraft had been based at Steeple Morden, the weather being appalling with severe thunderstorms, which was considered totally unfit for flying.

Düsseldorf was again the target on 10 September 1942 with thirteen Wellingtons allocated from 11 OTU, but only ten reached the target. Wellington DV930 crashed and burned at Chediston, Norfolk, killing all the crew; DV890 also failed to return. Three nights later, Bremen was the target with twelve Wellingtons dispatched from Bassingbourn and another five from Steeple Morden. The flak defences were very heavy with two aircraft from Steeple Morden lost. One of the Wimpys was damaged by flak and with reduced power was forced to crash land in enemy-occupied territory, the crew surviving without injury. With daylight approaching, the crew hid away and the following day split into two groups to evade capture. Unfortunately, all were captured to become POWs, although they had evaded capture for ten days despite being in flying gear.

The last bomber mission with 11 OTU at Bassingbourn and Steeple Morden was on 16 September with Essen the target. Nine Wellingtons were allocated—seven from Bassingbourn and two from Steeple Morden. The main target was the heavily defended Krupps Works. Sadly, three Wellingtons failed to return with the loss of the crews—a tragic end to 11 OTU's operations at the two stations. On 28 September, 11 OTU moved from 91 Group to 92 Group with the main base at Westcott and Satellite at Oakley. The move was completed by 2 October, with both original airfields to be allocated to the 8th USAAF with B-17s at Bassingbourn and Thunderbolts at Steeple Morden. During the stay at Bassingbourn and Steeple Morden, 11 OTU had trained hundreds of aircrew.

The strength at Westcott was forty-six Wellingtons. The unit used Mk Is, Mk IIIs, and Mk Xs—an example being Broughton-built Mk I DV778 KJ-A. Despite the overall reliability of the engines, by the time the aircraft had arrived at an OTU, they were very tired and engine problems caused a significant number of losses during training. As an example, 11 OTU lost on average nearly one aircraft a month, even when just operating in the local areas to the training stations. From November 1942 until April 1945, twenty-seven Wellingtons crashed, killing most of the crews, which consisted of novices under training as well as experienced instructors on 'rest tours'. Twelve of these losses were due to engine failures at a critical point of flight.

When 11 OTU was disbanded in 1945, 1,157 crews had been trained on around 121 courses at all four bases. No. 11 OTU was typical of the RAF Bomber Command operational training activities and illustrates the risks and challenges taken by the young aircrew of nineteen years old and above while under training.

No. 12 OTU was formed at Benson from 52 and 63 Squadrons along with C Flight of 12 Squadron as part of 6 Group with satellite at Mount Farm. By November 1940, it was at half strength with twenty-seven Wellingtons, achieving full strength by 1 December. In August 1941, a move was made to Chipping Warden with the full strength of fifty-four Wellingtons, plus other types, such as Ansons. Satellite airfields allocated were Gaydon, Turweston, and Edgehill. During 1942, like other OTUs, 12 OTU crews under training took part in Bomber Command raids. By 22 March 1945, there were thirty-nine Mk Xs on strength, but this was disbanded on 22 June 1945 having used Mk ICs, III, and X—an example being Blackpool-built Mk IC X3338 JP-P.

Training was often as hazardous as combat operations, especially on Nickel flights, dropping leaflets on enemy-occupied territory to help maintain the morale of the oppressed people. The Nickel flights were an introduction to operational flying in hopefully a more benign atmosphere, but sometimes, not all went as planned.

On the night of 13 July 1943, 12 OTU Wellington Mk III BJ702 took off from Chipping Warden with a trainee crew led by Wg Cdr Norman Bray. Soon after crossing the French coast, the port engine was hit by flak. Bray turned for home, but as he crossed back across the coast, the aircraft was hit again, damaging the wing, which made control difficult. With the aircraft in a gradual descent, it was obvious they would not make landfall in Britain, so Bray ordered the crew to prepare for ditching. Making a tail-down touchdown on the waves, the aircraft pitched forward, decelerating rapidly; this caused Bray to break his nose on the windscreen, but he was able to make a quick escape. Climbing out onto the wing, three crew members were already in the automatically inflated dinghy, but the front gunner's foot was trapped in the wreckage. Bray assisted his release and all were safe in the dinghy when the aircraft sank after fifteen minutes.

Despite being injured in the face, Bray was able to stem the blood flow while all the crew suffered from the cold and seasickness. With daylight, they were able to organise themselves and ration out water. Soon after 9 a.m., the French coast

Wellington B III Z1732 FQ-S from 12 OTU. (*BAE Systems*)

Wellington B III Z1792 FQ-J from 12 OTU. (*RAF Museum*)

near Le Havre was sighted. During the morning, they were circled by a Spitfire, but nothing followed. The crew kept paddling by day and overnight away from the French coast, and early the next morning, their flares were spotted by a group of Typhoons, who called in a 279 Squadron Hudson, which dropped a lifeboat. Meanwhile, air-sea rescue launches were alerted. After dropping the lifeboat successfully, the crew climbed aboard and headed for the English coast 80 miles away, escorted by four Typhoons. After four hours sailing towards England, they were intercepted by the ASR launches, this time escorted by Spitfires. The Wimpy crew were lifted out and fitted with dry clothing, with a return to Newhaven. Bray was treated for his badly broken nose and the crew members for a few cuts and bruises. Bray praised his young and inexperienced crew for them using their survival training they had received at Chipping Warden, which resulted in the safe return to their unit.

No. 14 OTU formed at Cottesmore 8 April 1940 as part of 6 Group with Hampdens, replaced from September to December 1942 by fifty Wellingtons together with Ansons and other support aircraft. Satellites were at Turweston and Edgehill to provide additional runways. A move was made to Market Harborough on 1 August 1943 with a satellite at Husbands Bosworth, and the OTU was disbanded on 24 June 1945. The OTU operated Mk ICs, IIIs, and Xs—an example being Broughton-built Mk X LP598 AM-S.

No. 15 OTU was formed in 6 Group from 75 and 48 Squadrons with a total of twenty-four Wellingtons at Harwell with a satellite at Hampstead Norris. As part of training, the crews participated in a leaflet raid on 18 July 1940, and from May 1941, the OTU was tasked with the training of crews for overseas squadrons. By June 1941, the full strength of fifty-four Wellingtons had been reached, and the OTU crews took part in seven major Bomber Command raids during 1942. The unit operated Mk IA, IC, II, III, X, and XVIIIs—an example being Weybridge-built Mk IC T2713 FH-T—and disbanded on 15 March 1944.

No. 16 OTU was formed as part of 6 Group from 7 and 76 Squadrons at Upper Heyford initially with Hampdens and Herefords. In April 1942, the unit converted to Wellingtons, taking part in Bomber Command raids, in addition to leaflet raids. The satellite was Barford St John, and by June 1942, the total establishment of Wellingtons was fifty-four with ten Ansons. The unit used Mk ICs, IIIs, and Xs—an example being Broughton-built Mk IC HE431 JS-P—and the OTU disbanded on 1 January 1945 to become a Mosquito training unit.

The last of the initial seven was 17 OTU within 6 Group, which formed at Upwood from 35 and 90 Squadrons with satellites at Warboys, Steeple Morden, and Polebrook, initially to train light bomber crews on Blenheims. A move was made to Silverstone on 17 April 1943 to become a three-quarters-strength OTU with a satellite at Turweston. By 3 July 1943, it had expanded to a full status of fifty-four Wellingtons. It was redesignated 201 AFS at Swinderby on 15 March 1947, by which time the Wellingtons had been withdrawn. The OTU operated Wellington ICs—an example being Weybridge-built T2606.

Wellington B IC L7850 VB-Y from 14 OTU after an irregular arrival. (*Newark Air Museum*)

Wellington B IC Z9103 with 15 OTU at Hampstead Norris in 1942. (*Newark Air Museum*)

An OTU course commenced with the pilot flying circuits and landings until he was qualified to go solo, followed by his flying being monitored by screen pilots. Each stage in the overall crew training was preceded by a day in ground school, followed by practicing what had been learned by day flying. The practical work consisted of formation flying and high-level bombing, with plenty of gunnery practice, often with experienced screen gunners, plus screen navigators, radio operators, and bomb aimers. The flying included cross-country navigation exercises, air-to-air and air-to-sea firing, and combat manoeuvres; the total flying time came to around thirty hours. Each OTU had support aircraft available, examples being Miles Masters for fighter affiliation, Martinets for towing target drogues, and Hurricanes to give experience of defending against attack from enemy fighters.

Having completed the first half of the course, the crews would go on leave, and the second half would be involved with night flying, again with circuits and landings plus cross-country exercises. The novice crew would complete their training by flying a diversionary 'Bullseyes' or 'Nickling' sorties to a relatively 'safe' target, where flak would be experienced for the first time. Following the OTU course, the crew would be posted to a gunnery flight equipped with Wellingtons, where some three hours would be flown on camera gun exercises, to hone accuracy.

No. 3 (Coastal) OTU formed at Chivenor on 27 November 1940 for the training of Anson and Beaufort crews with the expectation of re-equipping with Wellingtons and Whitleys. However, due to delays completing airfields, plans were changed with a move to Kinloss and then Silloth/Kirkbride until 29 July 1941 when there was a temporary move to Cranwell with the designation 3 OTU. Whitley training ceased in April 1943, and a move was made to Haverfordwest, training Wellington Leigh Light crews. No. 3 OTU disbanded on 4 January 1944, with Wellington training taken over by 6 OTU. Wellington Mk Is, IAs, ICs, IIIs, and VIIIs were used.

This massive training programme involved a considerable resource with the construction of the core airfields, some initially without runways. Accommodation had to be provided for the personnel on sites that were short term, rather than permanent stations used by the Bomber Command. Hangars and technical buildings were constructed, and runways were built together with connecting taxiways and aircraft dispersals with a form of air traffic control provided in a standard design watch office, many of which still exist on the old sites due to their solid concrete construction. The sites had to be secure with pill boxes and airfield defence anti-aircraft guns. Then there were experienced training crews on 'rest tours' from the main force, together with ground crew to maintain the sometimes-decrepit aircraft, which had done their fair share of arduous operations, been patched up from battle damage, and maintained in the open in all weathers.

Worn aircraft, novice aircrews, and the weather caused a high level of accidents with losses of experienced and training aircrew. Engine failure on take-off could be fatal for the crew, while hitting high ground in bad weather and mid-air collisions in closely spaced crowded airfield circuits were among the reasons for many losses. Wellingtons provided the background for Bomber Command training on all the major types, leaving Lancasters, Halifaxes, and Stirlings to receive ready trained crews in all the disciplines and only requiring conversion to type.

As Wellington production increased at the major factory units and more squadrons were formed, additional OTUs were opened, the next two on 27 May 1940 both within 6 Group. No. 19 OTU was formed at Kinloss equipped with Whitleys until 1944, when Wellingtons began to take their place in August. By 22 March 1945, there were thirty-six Mk IIIs and Xs on strength—an example being Blackpool-built Mk X NC740 UO-D—and the OTU disbanded on 26 June 1945. No. 20 OTU was based at Lossiemouth and by November was at half strength with twenty-seven Wellingtons. By January 1941, it had reached full strength with fifty-four Wellingtons, and then grew to 1.5 strength, with eighty-one Wellingtons. It reduced to fifty-five Wellingtons by March 1945, having used Mk IAs, ICs, IIIs, and Xs—an example being Weybridge-built Mk IC Z8981 JM-A.

No. 18 OTU was formed within 6 Group with Battles at Hucknall to train Polish crews. It moved to Bramcote on 7 November 1940 as half an OTU with twenty-seven Wellingtons, growing through 1941 to a full OTU status and by April 1942 had fifty-four Wellingtons. It then reduced in size in stages, and on 11 May 1942, 6 Group became 91 Group, the OTU flying on six major Bomber Command raids. On 1 September 1942, it became part of 93 Group, and on 27 October 1942, the Polish Flight went to 6 OTU at Thornaby, leaving 18 OTU at half strength with twenty-seven Wellingtons. On 27 March, a move was made to Finningley, returning to full status in early 1944. On 20 October 1944, it rejoined 91 Group with a strength of fifty-four Wellingtons having flown Mk As, ICs, IIIs, IVs, and Xs—an example being Broughton-built Mk X LN184 D. The unit disbanded on 30 January 1945.

The early OTUs were equipped with different bomber types according to what crews would be flying on operations. However, with the entry into service of the new four-engined bombers, it was realised that to introduce new crews to Stirlings, Halifaxes, or Lancasters was going to be too much of a challenge in one go. It was therefore decided to retain the basic night bomber training with the twin-engined Wellington, of which there were plenty available, and introduce an additional step in the training programme with a heavy conversion unit (HCU) to familiarise with the bigger aircraft. This also allowed more of the bigger bomber production to be allocated to operational bomber squadrons, making the Wellington the predominant OTU aircraft.

Five more Wellington Bomber OTUs were formed in 1941. The first that year was 21 OTU in 6 Group at Moreton-in-Marsh on 21 January, with training starting on 3 March. There were satellites at Edgehill, Enstone, and Honeybourne. By August, there was a full complement of fifty-four Wellingtons, and crews from the OTU took part in seven Bomber Command raids during 1942. By 22 March 1945, the Wellington numbers had reduced to thirty-nine Mks ICs, IIIs, and Xs—an example being Blackpool-built Mk X ME976.

A move was made to Finningley on 25 November 1946, and it was redesignated 202 AFS on fifteen March 1947 when it was operating eleven Wellington T 10s, providing multi-engine aircrew training, increasing to seventeen Mk 10s by December 1947—an example being NA791 FME-J. The unit disbanded into 201 AFS at Swinderby on 1 December 1947. Also formed at Finningley in 7 Group was 25 OTU on 1 March 1941, initially training with Hampdens, but by May, there were twenty-four Wellingtons, thirty-six in November, and by April 1942, the full complement of fifty-four Wellingtons had been delivered. There were satellites in Balderton and Bircotes.

The crews took part in Bomber Command raids, and by 1 September 1942, it had reduced to three-quarters establishment, and it operated the standard mix of Mks ICs, IIIs, and Xs—an example being Broughton-built Mk III BK179 ZP-Y. Flying ceased on 7 January 1943, and it disbanded on 1 February. Next to form was 23 OTU at Pershore in 6 Group on 1 April 1941, and by August, it had received fifty-four Wellingtons with satellites at Defford and Stratford.

Crews flew on Bomber Command raids during 1942, plus leaflet raids as part of the training. By June 1942, the establishment had reduced to two-thirds status with thirty-six Wellingtons and operated Mk ICs, IIIs, and Xs—an example being Blackpool-built Mk IC X3172 G3. Disbandment came on 15 March 1944.

No 22 OTU formed at Wellesbourne Mountford in 6 Group on 14 April with satellites at Stratford and Gaydon; by August, it had fifty-four Wellingtons, which had grown to 1¼ status with sixty-six Wellingtons by August 1942. By February 1943, the establishment had returned to fifty-four with mainly RCAF crews being trained. In September 1944, there were eighty-one Wellingtons on charge, which reduced to forty-two by March 1945, with disbandment on 24 July 1945. Versions used were Mk ICs, IIIs, and Xs—an example being Broughton-built Mk IC X9791 DD-D.

The final Bomber Command OTU to form in 1941 was No. 27 within 6 Group at Litchfield on 23 April with satellites at Tatenhill and Church Broughton. Initial equipment was fifty-four Mk ICs by August and was mainly used to train RAAF crews, and 117 sorties were made on Bomber Command raids in 1942. By October 1942, Mk IIIs had been received with a total of fifty-four aircraft, and in August 1943, Mk Xs began to arrive—an example being Blackpool-built Mk X JA341 UJ-T. The unit disbanded on 22 June 1945.

Despite strong Wellington geodetic structure, there were examples of structural failure, particularly with aircraft that had been flying on demanding operations. Starting on 24 May 1942, the first of around twenty losses was T2802 of 1483 Flt during a fighter evasion exercise when the wing failed. Others included on 29 August 1943 Mk III BK431 with 29 OTU; the port wing failed upwards during a fighter affiliation exercise, killing all on board. On investigation, it was found the bolts holding the lower port wing spar had failed due to metal fatigue. In a subsequent investigation by Vickers, two main causes were identified. It was found that the detail design of the spar boom joint was faulty and the material used in the manufacture had high levels of tensile stress, both encouraging fatigue failure.

No. 27 OTU Wellington on approach to Litchfield. (*Newark Air Museum*)

The solution was to redesign the spar boom joint using improved steel, which was approved in July 1944.

Another five night bomber crew training OTUs were formed in 1942, the first being 26 OTU as part of 7 Group on 15 January on a three-quarter strength status with twenty-seven Wellingtons. Satellite airfields used were Cheddington and Little Horwood, with the crews taking part in Bomber Command raids during 1942. By February 1943, fifty-four Wellingtons were on strength, the types used being the usual mix of Mk ICs, IIIs, and Xs—an example being Broughton-built Mk IC DV725 J. The OTU disbanded on 4 March 1946.

No. 24 OTU formed at Honeybourne in 7 Group on 15 March, initially with two-thirds status, growing to the full status of fifty-four Wellingtons by September and specialised in training RCAF crews. By March 1945, it was down to forty-five

Wellingtons, the types being Mk IIIs and X—an example being Broughton-built Mk X LP355 FB-S. The unit disbanded on 24 July 1945.

No. 29 OTU formed at North Luffenham within 7 Group on 21 April with crew training commencing in June with 27 Wellingtons. Satellites were at Woolfox Lodge and Bruntingthorpe. OTU crews participated in four major Bomber Command raids during 1942, and by December, the full strength of fifty-four Wellingtons had been achieved. By February 1943, there were still fifty-four Mk IIIs in service, but in March 1945, the strength had reduced to ¾ status with thirty-one Mk Xs; Mk XIIIs were also on strength. An example was Broughton-built Mk III BK444 NT-A and the unit disbanded on 27 May 1945.

No. 28 OTU formed at Wymeswold in 92 Group on 16 May 1942 with Mk ICs initially at half strength. A satellite was at Castle Donington. The crews took part in some Bomber Command raids during 1942 with twenty-seven Wellingtons in July. In November, the status had increased to ¾ with forty Wellingtons, and by January 1943, it was at full status with fifty-four Wellingtons. By March 1944, the OTU was fully equipped with Mk IIIs and Xs—an example being Broughton-built Mk IC DV824 LB-Q. The unit disbanded on 15 October 1944.

No. 30 OTU Formed at Hixton on 28 June in 93 Group with satellite airfield at Deighford. The first of the initial twenty-seven Wellingtons was delivered on 23 July, and OTU crews flew on a number of Bomber Command raids during 1942. By December 1942, the full complement of fifty-four Wellingtons had been supplied, and by February 1944, it consisted of thirty-five Mk IIIs and fifteen Mk Xs, replacing the earlier Mk ICs. In October 1944, the status was reduced to ¾ strength with forty Wellingtons, and a move was made to Gamston in 91 Group on 2 February 1945. By March 1945, strength had been reduced to twenty-nine Wellingtons, and the unit was disbanded on 12 June 1945. An example of the Wellingtons with the unit was Broughton-built Mk X LP116 BT-M.

In addition to the night bomber OTUs, there were three more specialist units created in 1942, 62 OTU being formed at Usworth on 1 June 1942 to train radio observers initially with Ansons. On 8 August 1944, C Flt was formed for GEE training, and from March 1945, the first of twenty-nine Wellington Mk XVII and XVIII radar trainers were delivered—an example being Blackpool-built Mk XVIII ND113 '27'. Flying ceased on 14 May 1945 and the unit disbanded on 6 June, Woolsington being used as a satellite.

No. 81 OTU was formed as part of 93 Group at Ashbourne on 10 July 1942 with half strength of Whitleys, moving to Tilstock on 1 September 1942 with a satellite airfield at Sleap. From November 1944, Wellington Mk Xs were received for transport aircrew training. By January 1945, there were fifty-one Wellingtons, and it was redesignated 1380 (Transport Support) Conversion Unit on 10 August 1945—an example being Broughton-built Mk X NA962 EZ-H. Soon after being designated 1380 CU, the need for transport crews declined and it was disbanded on 21 January 1946.

No. 111 OTU was formed at Nassau, Bahamas, on 20 August 1942 to train reconnaissance crews on American-built aircraft. It began to depart to Britain

No. 30 OTU Wellington B IIIs, including BK347 BT-Z at Hixon being prepared for the next sorties. (*RAF Museum*)

on 25 July 1945, reopening at Lossiemouth within 17 Group on coastal training duties on 1 August 1945 equipped with twenty-five Liberators and seven Wellington Mk XIIIs and XIVs. It moved to the control of 18 Group with a satellite at Milltown. In November, the status was reduced to eight Liberators and three Wellingtons—an example being Blackpool-built Mk XVIII PG183 X3-CC. The unit disbanded on 21 May 1946.

No. 6 OTU was formed at Sutton Bridge on 6 March 1940 for fighter training but reformed on 19 July 1941 as 6 (Coastal) OTU at Thornaby equipped with Hudsons. In October 1942, the unit had re-equipped with twenty-two Wellington Mk XIVs and twenty Mk ICs, in addition to the Czech Operational Training Flight. It changed from Bomber Command to Coastal Command on 27 February 1943, moving to Silloth on 10 March 1943. By August 1943, it had twenty-five Mk VIIIs, XIs, and XIIIs for the training of GR crews at home and overseas, plus the Leigh Light squadrons. By March 1944, it had a mix of ten Mk ICs, IIIs, and Xs, in addition to three Mk XIIIs, later adding twenty Mk XIIs and Mk XIVs. The unit moved to Kinloss on 18 July 1945 and started Lancaster courses in July 1946. An example was Weybridge-built Wellington Mk XIII MP581 74.

With Wellingtons withdrawn from Bomber Command operations, the aircraft were used in a wide range of training roles during 1943. On 12 March, 104 OTU was formed within 44 Group at Nutts Corner, Belfast, equipped with twenty-seven Wellington to train transport crews and was disbanded on 5 February 1944. On 5 April, 105 OTU was formed within 44 Group at Bramcote for the training of airline crews, equipped initially with fifty-four Wellington Mk ICs fitted with Warwick controls. In September 1944, Dakotas began to replace the Wellingtons—an example being Blackpool-built Mk X MF521 8F-R.

Three more operational training units were formed in 1943 to expand the training of Bomber Command heavy night bomber crews. No. 82 OTU formed on 1 June at Ossington within 93 Group from part of 28 OTU with fifty-four Wellingtons, with the first intake of crews arriving on 23 June. By August, there were twelve Mk IIIs and twenty-five Mk Xs, and the strength was reduced to ¾ status on 15 June 1944, followed by disbandment on 9 January 1945.

No. 83 OTU formed as part of 93 Group at Child's Ercall/Peplow from 30 OTU at ¾ strength with forty Wellingtons by June 1944. The unit operated Mk IIIs and Xs—an example being Broughton-built Mk III BK151 GS-A. It was disbanded on 28 October 1944. No. 84 OTU formed on 1 September as part of 92 Group at Desborough with fifty-four Wellingtons. It was reduced to ¾ strength on 9 May 1944 and operated Mk IIIs and Xs—an example being Broughton-built Mk X LN175 IF-F. The unit was disbanded on 14 June 1945.

Also in 1943, 63 OTU formed on 7 September within 9 Group at Honiley to train night fighter crews. By September, ten Wellington classroom trainers had been delivered, consisting of Mk XIs and Mk XVIIs—an example being Weybridge-built Mk XI MP523. The unit disbanded on 21 March 1944, with the Wellingtons going to 51 OTU. The final OTU formed in 1943 was 76 OTU on 1 October at Aqir in Egypt to train night bomber crews for operations in the Middle East. There were forty Mk ICs, IIIs, and Xs—an example being Blackpool-built Mk III HF526 F. The unit disbanded on 30 July 1945.

On the first day of January 1944, 77 OTU formed within 203 Group at Qastina with Wellingtons for the training of SAAF night bomber aircrew with twenty-one Wellingtons. The unit operated a mix of Mk ICs, IIIs, VIIIs, Xs, and XIVs—an example being Broughton-built Mk X LN501 N. Flying ceased on 18 June 1945, and the unit was formally disbanded on 9 July. For specialist aircrew training in ASV radar and Leigh Light operation, 78 OTU was formed at Ein Shemer, commencing on 14 February 1944, equipped with fifty-four Wellingtons. It was equipped with Mk IIIs, VIIIs, Xs, XIIs, XIIIs, and XIVs—an example being Blackpool-built Mk X JA178. Flying ceased on 28 June 1945, followed by disbandment on 23 July.

In 1944, there was still a need for training more night bomber crews to replace the continuing losses. On 15 June, 85 OTU was formed within 92 Group at Husbands Bosworth from part of 14 OTU at ¾ strength with forty Wellington Mk IIIs and Xs—an example being Broughton-built Mk X LN758. The unit disbanded on 14 June 1945. Also on 15 June, 86 OTU was formed as part of 93 Group at Gamston from part of 82 OTU with a ¾ strength of forty-nine Wellington Mk IIIs and Xs—an example being Broughton-built Mk X HE485 B. It was disbanded on 15 October 1944.

The Central Gunnery School (CGS) was formed on 6 November 1939 at Warmwell as part of 25 Group. The main requirement was to improve and upgrade the standards of RAF air gunnery. The role of the CGS was to provide post-operational training for air gunners and fighter pilots, the students having already proved themselves in combat and demonstrated sufficient success to warrant an advanced course in gunnery. The course lasted one month and consisted of ten fighter pilots and thirty-two air gunners, with a 50 per cent overlap resulting in double that number serving on the station at any one time.

The CGS moved to Castle Kennedy on 23 June 1941, at Chelveston on 5 December 1941, and at Sutton Bridge on 1 April 1942, where Wellington Mk Is, IA/Cs, and IIIs became part of the mixed collection of RAF fighters and bombers on the airfield. It was logical to combine both bomber and fighter gunnery instruction as they were complimentary for combat training. The fighter gunnery training was headed by the famous South African fighter ace, 'Sailor' Malan while the Bomber Wing was led initially by Wg Cdr J. M. Warfield, who was succeeded on 25 June by Wg Cdr J. J. Sutton, an experienced bomber pilot. The main task of the unit was to train gunnery instructors to serve with operational squadrons and training units, with responsibility for all aspects of tactical gunnery. These air gunner instructors were responsible for maintaining a high standard of marksmanship; to improve the operational efficiency of air gunners, by maintaining their morale and fitness; to start and control gunnery training, and aircraft recognition; to ensure gun turret maintenance and harmonisation; to advise on the use of gunnery equipment; to support squadron and flight commanders on disciplinary action; and to define the principles of air fighting tactics.

The Wellingtons were training work horses, with initially some thirty combat-weary early Mk Is. Each bomber would have four trainees on board, with each aerial training session lasting for about an hour. The initial exercise was on range estimation, followed by quarter attacks and then all aspects attacks. Later stages involved full evasive flying of the bomber with fighters from all directions. While most combat training was at 3,000 feet, there were also low-level attacks at high closing speeds, making them hazardous and relying on the fighter pilot breaking away in good time from a head-on attack. Exercises also involved firing at towed targets by Henleys and Lysanders.

Training was intensive and demanding to prepare the gunners for active combat; the trainee air gunners were supervised by a fire controller who was under the Wellington astrodome. He controlled the aircraft gunners and also the pilot on evasive actions, while the instructor controlling the exercise would be in the right-hand pilot's seat next to the captain. Among the violent manoeuvres was the bomber corkscrew when the Wellington was often subject to two or three g, testing the strength of the geodetic structure to its limit. As the exercises had to be as realistic as possible, there were risks of collision, and most of the training was over the ranges in the Wash or surrounding the Fens. Maintenance was challenging with some sixty various aircraft based at Sutton Bridge, and in the winter weather, it was sometimes only possible to make twenty serviceable, especially with the poor condition of the Wimpys.

Wellington B IA N2887 from 5 CGS on fighter affiliation exercise with a Spitfire and Mustang. (*RAF Museum*)

Wellington B IA N2887 from 5 CGS with a Spitfire IIA on fighter affiliation. (*BAE Systems*)

Rather than use real ammunition, results were assessed by the use of camera guns, which were reviewed after each sortie, with flying training complemented by ground training involving theory of ballistics, discussions of tactics, and—most important—aircraft recognition. As part of deflection training, clay pigeon shooting was introduced.

As with the Wellington OTUs, the CGS was also subjected to the ultimate operational training by being allocated to the 1,000 bomber raids in May 1942. The war-weary Wimpys were early combat veterans and apart from being unable to sustain long periods of flying were lacking in suitable combat equipment, which would have been donated to the operational fleet. As a result, only three CGS Wellingtons could be made available to take part in the 1,000 bomber raid to Cologne and back. The three aircraft were detached to Feltwell for operational co-operation with Bomber Command, complete with air and ground crews. Out of the total of 1,047 bombers despatched on the raid, forty-one were lost, of which one was a CGS veteran N2849, which had served with 149 Squadron at the start of the war. Four of the six crew were CGS experienced staff members.

As with all the training units, accidents were not uncommon, mainly due to the poor state of the Wellingtons and collisions. On 6 July 1942, Mk I L7774 had the port engine fail on the way to the Wash ranges, which caught fire. With the aircraft in a gradual descent, there was no possibility of returning to base, so a forced-landing was made on farmland. The crew managed to scramble clear with minor injuries before the wreck went up in flames. On 13 August 1943, Spitfire P7530 and Wellington P9228 collided near Lakenheath, killing six crew with two survivors. The aircraft were practicing air-to-air combat and the Spitfire hit the Wellington, losing its port wing; it spun into the ground inverted, with the Wellington crashing nearby.

RAF Sutton Bridge was always under review due to the small size of the airfield, which could get water-logged, and restricted accommodation. Its main advantage was being located close to the ranges, but after two years, the CGS moved to Catfoss in Yorkshire on 24 February 1944. A final move was made to Leconfield on 12 November 1945, and on 30 December 1946, there were still nine Wellington Xs on the strength, together with Mosquito VIs, Spitfire XVIs, and Meteor IIIs. The Central Gunnery School was finally disbanded 31 December 1954, replaced by the Fighter Weapons School and the Coastal Command Gunnery School.

Wellingtons therefore played not only a vital role in the earlier Bomber Command offensives against Germany, but also was the backbone of training night bomber and other crews. Its rugged design and strong structure gave it undemanding flying qualities. allowing novice crews to concentrate on the vital task of delivering bombs to the enemy, for a number of years the only form of direct retaliation.

5

Wellingtons in the Mediterranean

Weather conditions in the Mediterranean were generally an improvement over northern Europe, as well as ground-based anti-aircraft defences being less intense, making Wellingtons more effective in combat. Yet it was no walk in the park. German and Italian fighter defences were more than adequate, and the hot climate with sand and dust caused their own difficulties, particularly with wear and tear to engines and other mechanical systems.

The first Wellingtons deployed to the theatre were with 1 GRU tasked with minesweeping Allied harbours. The first aircraft departed Britain on 20 May 1940 in groups of two or three, making refuelling stops at Luqa in Malta and Mersa Matruh, safely arriving at their base at Ismailia after three days. Due to local climate conditions, it was necessary to install additional generator coolers, which delayed the start of operations until 14 June, with the first sweep of Alexandria harbour at a height of between 40 and 50 feet. Trials followed to determine the most effective way of sweeping the vital 87-mile Suez Canal, and although this could be achieved by a single aircraft, it was more effective to operate with a pair of aircraft flying a few miles apart.

Four Wimpys were detached in January 1941 to Capuzzo in Libya to sweep the approaches to Tobruk harbour, but they were recalled to Ismailia after a few days to clear German mines. During the first sortie on 1 February, two mines were exploded. Although the Royal Navy believed they were the experts at minesweeping, the Suez Canal could be cleared much more rapidly from the air.

Later on 1 February, Wellingtons more than earned their keep. The large 25,000-ton liner *Dominion Monarch* was proceeding carefully along the canal, its bulk filling the space available on its way to the Great Bitter Lake. Two Wellingtons were sweeping the waters ahead of the ship and one aircraft had turned back towards the ship. At a speed of 130 mph and 50 feet above the water, the pilot of L7771 was approaching the enormous ship; just as he pulled up to avoid hitting the bows, there was a violent explosion, knocking the DWI operator off his seat by the impact. A large mine had been exploded a short distance from the approaching ship, but the vessel was saved undamaged. If it had been sunk, the lifeline waterway link between the Mediterranean and Indian Ocean would have been blocked for at least three months, meaning all shipping would have to follow the hazardous route round the Cape of Good Hope to connect the Atlantic with Asia.

Only one aircraft was lost during these operations, when P2518 suffered an engine failure on 9 February 1943, and the pilot was forced to belly-land in the desert, as when fitted with the DWI loop, it could not continue to fly on one engine. Routine sweeping of the Suez Canal continued for the remainder of 1 GRU existence with regular deployments to sweep Tobruk harbour as the land battle moved back and forth along the North African desert. The unit was finally disbanded in March 1944, the remaining aircraft being struck off charge in July.

The bombing war in the Mediterranean was in three basic phases. The initial threat was caused by Italy declaring war on the Allies in support of Hitler, requiring RAF reinforcements in the area. The second phase was the bombing of Rommel's *Afrika Korps* along North Africa, as well as supply shipping. The final phase was in support of the Allied invasion and advances through Italy into southern European.

When Italy declared war on 10 June 1940, the only RAF bombers available were Blenheims and Wellesleys, while 216 Squadron was equipped with obsolete Bombay bomber-transports, and 70 Squadron had even older Valentias. With an urgent requirement to provide bomber capability against Italian threats in both East and North Africa, 70 Squadron moved to Kabrit in Egypt on 9 September

Wellington DW 1 L4356 in the defence of the Suez Canal against magnetic mines. (*BAE Systems*)

1940 and began to re-equip with Wellington ICs during the month. To increase strength further, 37 and 38 Squadrons were transferred out of Bomber Command in November, the former being based at Luqa, Malta, from 13 November 1940, and the latter to Ismailia in Egypt on 24 November, both operating Mk ICs.

The initial challenge for aircrew was ferrying the aircraft from home airfields to their new bases, but the starting point was moved to an airfield in south-west England, with Portreath in Cornwall being typical. With the German occupation of France, the most direct route was cut off, and all flights had to route across the inhospitable Bay of Biscay to Gibraltar, keeping well clear of neutral Portugal and Spain. Some flights had sufficient range to overfly Gibraltar and head direct for Malta, the flight time being around eight hours.

One of the 37 Squadron Wimpys, CV645, was taken by a crew straight out of training at 15 OTU at Harwell to Egypt via Gibraltar, departing from Portreath via Lyneham. The take-off time was 6.57 a.m., the aircraft carrying two overload fuel tanks. Initially, the weather was poor but cleared off the Portuguese coast, and a landing was made at Gibraltar after nine hours and twenty-five minutes with strong head winds. The next day, briefing was in the morning ready for a departure at 3.45 p.m. and with favourable winds heading for Malta, landing safely with no enemy raid in progress. Following a briefing for the captain and

Servicing a 37 Squadron Wellington in the desert. (*BAE Systems*)

No. 38 Squadron Wellington after a forced-landing by the bomb dump at LG09 in October 1941. (*RAF Museum*)

Wellington B IC Z8787 J from 37 Squadron on LG60 in December 1941. (*RAF Museum*)

Wellington B IC R1033 D from 38 Squadron at Sidi Assiz in April 1941. (*RAF Museum*)

Wellington B IC of 38 Squadron with nose art at LG09 in North Africa in 1941. (*RAF Museum*)

rapid refreshments by the aircraft, they were refuelled and airborne again within fifty-five minutes. They headed 24 degrees east with the morning star ahead and were fired upon when close to Benghazi, passing Mersa on time finally reaching the landing ground at 6.30 a.m. the next day. The bonus for the new crew was being credited with three operations and twenty-five combat hours—a positive start to their tour.

The hazardous deployment to the Mediterranean theatre was not without its losses, with ferry training units established from 1941 to better prepare the often novice crews for the arduous flight. Crews were attached to the ferry training units for the duration of the flight to the final destination, each aircraft being prepared for the ferry flight with additional fuel tanks. The aircraft they ferried may not have been the one allocated for their combat duties after arrival. An additional hazard was from time to time the aircraft were sabotaged during refuelling at Malta, one aircraft suffering engine failure after take-off and ditching in the sea just off the North African coast, with the crew swimming ashore to be taken prisoner. A similar loss was Mk IC W5677, which departed Luqa on 9 April 1941 and ditched near Apollonia due to water in the tanks. This was followed later by Mk III DF689 of 70 Squadron, which force-landed due to engine failure on 3 June 1943 after a bombing operation to railway yards at Messina. The aircraft was damaged, and the crew was unhurt.

The runway at Gibraltar was only 1,200 yards long, making arrivals challenging. Departing from Portreath in January 1943, Mk III HF750 flew without a stop to

Wellington B IC Z9020 C in the North African desert. (*RAF Museum*)

Wellington GR VIII T2998 after crash landing at LG09 in North Africa. (*RAF Museum*)

Gibraltar, touching down right on the threshold to avoid running off the other end into the sea. They managed to stop before the end after eight hours and five minutes in the air, half of the time at night. After a rest day, the departure was before dawn with extra fuel, heading south to the Atlas Mountains over the featureless Sahara Desert to avoid hostilities in Tunisia and turning east towards Libya. After ten hours and thirty minutes in the air, they landed at Benina, inland from Benghazi, joining the other parked Wellingtons. After waiting for two days, the crew flew on to 70 Squadron at El Magrun, qualifying for fifteen hours and thirty minutes operational flying.

Wellington Mk IC SV419 departed Portreath on 8 January 1942, making a successful arrival at Gibraltar, to find they were the subject of an experiment to fly direct to Benghazi without the refuelling stop at Luqa, avoiding the risk of an air raid on arrival. A long, cylindrical, 250-gallon fuel tank was fitted down the centre of the aircraft, with the additional weight making the take-off demanding. On leaving the end of the runway, the pilot raised the undercarriage, flying straight and level without hitting the sea.

As the fuel in the wing tanks reduced, the decision was made to start a transfer from the overload tank, which, if there was a problem, still allowed a safe landing at Malta, which was passed to port. The front gunner had the task of the manual transfer, sitting in the cold, dark, and draughty area behind the wing main spar. Using a torch, the captain read the instructions over the intercom for the opening and closing the valves in the correct order, following which the fuel had to be hand pumped, with the fuel indication showing a modest gain. The instruction was to keep pumping until all the usable fuel was transferred, although the navigator had his doubts about reaching the destination. After eleven hours and fifty minutes, the aircraft had not reached land, and the fuel gauges were showing empty. Five minutes later with the engines at low power, a beach was sighted, the pilot lowering the flaps and undercarriage, landing safely on a firm surface parallel to the water.

The captain and front gunner decided to go inland and see what habitation was available, following an easterly track, continuing all day without food and water. At 4 p.m., after being on the go for thirty-two hours, a truck appeared coming towards them. As it came closer, it was possible to see two soldiers on board, who fired a machine gun over the aircrew's heads. The pilot and gunner raised their hands in surrender, to find the soldiers were Sikhs in the 4th Indian Division of the 8th Army, who rescued the RAF crew members. The rest of the crew were recovered from the beach and spent a week in Barca, Libya, which had previously been occupied by the German army. With the main street full of vehicles going towards Alexandria, it was realised there was a retreat in progress, and a SAAF tanker was in the traffic. Persuading the driver to go to the stranded Wellington, rather than destroy it, the remaining 200 gallons was transferred to the aircraft. The aircraft was still parked on the beach undamaged, the refuelling being through funnels at four gallons at a time; by early afternoon, there were only 30 gallons in each tank, with German advances expected at any time. The pilots decided to attempt a take-off with the remainder of the crew going back to Barca in the tanker. By powering up the engines, the aircraft came out of the ruts, and after many bumps, it unbelievably became airborne and landed at Barca to fully refuel, leaving the next morning for Cairo via Mersa Matruh. The aircraft had flown 3,500 miles in 28.5 hours over an elapsed time of twenty-four days, but arrived fully serviceable ready for combat. Sadly, the aircraft was lost with its crew two months after arriving in Egypt during an anti-shipping operation on 5 April when serving with 38 Squadron.

Initial bombing operations were against the Italian army based in Libya, which invaded Egypt on 10 September 1940. The major targets were supply ports and supporting airfields. The first night bombing attack was against the port of Benghazi by 70 Squadron on 19 September. Malta was also a base for 148 Squadron, where the Italian navy base at Naples was within range, and where on 14 December a jetty and battleship were both hit and damaged. The Naples docks were bombed again on 29 December, and on 8 January 1941, a cruiser was bombed in Palermo harbour. Although flak at Naples was fierce, coming up from the surrounding harbour as well as the enemy ships, it was fortunately was not too accurate. The enemy airfield at Castel Benito was attacked at 200 feet, with the regular tidy lines of Italian aircraft being easily machine gunned.

In January, an attack was made on Tripoli power station and fuel storage facility, dive bombing from 1,000 feet at 310 mph, hitting railway installations. On 15 January, the unpopular Catania was targeted, which became more hazardous after German aircraft took over from the Italians. The port of Valentia was bombed by 70 Squadron on 7 November 1940 with the loss of two Wellingtons to defending Italian fighters.

During the first few weeks of being based in Malta, the Wimpys were operated by the Wellington Flight until the reforming of 148 Squadron on 1 December 1940. Two aircraft from the Wellington Flight were lost when they had engine failure on take-off, caused the aircraft to hit local high ground, killing most of the crew. In early 1941, heavy enemy attacks by both the Italians and Germans started, with seven Wellingtons destroyed on the ground—one from 70 Squadron and six from 148 Squadron. The plan was to detach Wellingtons from 148 Squadron from Egypt to Luqa with each aircraft flying three sorties a night against the well-defended Sicilian airfield of Comiso in an effort to reduce enemy attacks on Malta.

In support of the faltering Italian campaign, General Erwin Rommel was sent with an initial small Panzer force in March 1941, supported by an increased strength of Luftwaffe bomber and fighter units. This was the start of a major *Afrika Korps* campaign, which moved to and fro along the North African desert between Libya and Egypt lasting over two years. An additional complication for Allied forces was a pro-Nazi coup in Iraq that threatened oil supplies. The RAF base of Habbaniya was under siege by Iraqi troops, and in response, detachments of Wellingtons were made from 37 and 70 Squadrons to Shaibah. From here, the

Wellington B IC T2818 T from Malta Flight at Luqa in 1940. (*RAF Museum*)

surrounding troops were attacked, with the emergency being over by the end of the month.

In the Western Desert, an early change to the RAF bomber organisation was the formation of 205 (Heavy Bomber) Group at Shallufa near Suez on 23 October 1941. This group took control of all Wellington squadrons in the region until the end of the war, by which time the headquarters had moved to Foggia in Italy. With rapid front-line changes, bombing operations were very fluid, with moves over many landing grounds. As well as supporting Allied armies with the bombing of enemy supply lines and installations, there were also frequent attacks on Tobruk and Benghazi.

Operations to Benghazi became frequent and often hazardous during 1941 and 1942, particularly for 70 Squadron with eight operations during July 1941, the round trip taking over nine hours, involving both bombing and mine-laying. Following a raid on the night of 1–2 November 1941, five Wellingtons with 148 Squadron crash-landed in the desert when they ran out of fuel due to LG 104 at Qotafiyah II being fogbound, fortunately without loss of life.

On 25 February 1942, on a mine-laying operation, one aircraft was lost when it force-landed near El Adem with the six crew members safe and able to return to their squadron. With the German invasion of Crete in May 1941, 148 Squadron Wellington W5555 was tasked with dropping supplies to Allied troops stranded in the mountains on 2 March 1942. On the return, the starboard engine caught fire, which the pilot managed to extinguish and feather the propeller. The crew dumped everything movable to lighten the weight, but the aircraft was still forced to ditch about 8 miles off the Egyptian coast, and the crew were rescued by an ASR launch after eight hours in a dinghy, returning to their base at Kabrit by train after landing at Alexandria.

Living and operational conditions in the desert were very challenging, both for air and ground crews. Living conditions were very basic with no permanent accommodation, resulting in the use of tents in the sand. Beds were made from wood scavenged from packing cases and any other available timber. Parachutes were used as pillows and flying jackets as blankets in the cold desert nights. There were flies everywhere, making eating unpleasant, and water was rationed to a gallon a day for everything.

Working conditions were worse for the ground crews, with no shelter for the aircraft, and working inside the aircraft during the day when the outside temperature was close to 50 degrees Celsius. In addition to high temperatures, wear and tear on the aircraft caused by the sand made serviceability challenging, with all repair and servicing at a minimal level, particularly when deployed away from major airfields to desert relief landing grounds. Any major servicing was undertaken in Cairo with Wellingtons having to be ferried from as far afield as Malta. In contrast to the heat and dust, when it did rain in the desert, airfields were turned into swamps with mud everywhere, requiring PSP metal sheeting to be laid to allow operations to continue.

An advantage of the North African terrain was that there were plenty of places to make a safe forced-landing without harm to the crew and often the aircraft. Wellington IC DV457 had to make a forced-landing on 9 July 1942 behind enemy lines following a raid on Tobruk due to a shortage of fuel. After sending SOS messages, they were picked up by a 216 Squadron Bombay, which brought in a repair team to rectify some minor damage and refuel the aircraft in less than four hours, followed by a successful recovery. This was just one example of a number of similar cases. An even more challenging recovery was when Mk IC Z8787 lost its port propeller during an operation against Benghazi on the night of 27–28 May 1942, resulting in a wheels-up landing removing large areas of the fuselage underside. Led by Clive Stanbury of 70 Squadron, a team of volunteers used a captured German lorry loaded with a replacement propeller and undercarriage parts, driving 200 miles behind enemy lines to carry out emergency repairs, allowing Stanbury to take-off as enemy troops were approaching, taking it to LG 104 at Qotafiyah II. For this act, Stanbury was awarded the DSO.

One of the targets for 37 Squadron in 1942 was the Italian-occupied Greek island of Rhodes—specifically, the military airfield at Maritsa. This was the main one of three military airfields on Rhodes, located around 8.5 miles south-west of Rhodes Town. While bombing the airfield, the Wellingtons were attacked by defending CR 42s. Maritsa was the only permanent air base on the island and after the war became the international airport, but due to challenging approaches to the runways, it was replaced in 1977 by the new airport.

One of the major threats to RAF bombing operations was the Luftwaffe night fighters based in Sicily, initially at Catania, before moving to the Libyan coast at Derna. *Hauptmann* Heinz Rokker shot down five 205 Group Wellingtons during the month of June 1942 by which time Rommel's *Afrika Korps* had occupied Tobruk and were advancing to the east. During the night of 26–27 June, Rokker flying a Ju 88CV-6 shot down DV522 of 37 Squadron, which was bombing weapons stores at Via Balbia, with the aircraft force-landing in the desert; the five surviving crew members walked for three hours to Allied lines. A second Wellington credited to Rokker that night was 70 Squadron's DV564, which belly-landed at LG 104 with the second pilot and wireless operator wounded and rear gunner killed.

The next night, RAF Wellingtons were bombing the German-occupied Mersa Matruh, and Rokker fired at R1029 of 108 Squadron, causing the starboard engine to burst into flames, slowing it down dramatically. The Ju 88 flew alongside the Wellington, from which he received return fire, injuring both the pilot and radar operator, with the Wellington making a belly-landing at Amriya; the crew was safe.

A month later on 28 July, 70 Squadron's HX364 was part of a bombing attack on Tobruk harbour and brought down in the sea, the crew being rescued by an Italian ship. Three crew members were later drowned when the ship was sunk by a Royal Navy submarine on 17 August. It was not until 18 April 1943 that Rokker shot down Luqa-based HX487 of 221 Squadron near Masala; the aircraft crashed in the sea with the loss of the entire crew. Apart from the last aircraft, many of the aircrew survived—a testament to the rugged construction of the Wellington, despite sustaining major damage, usually to the engines.

Plt Off. Hunter and his crew delivered Wellington Mk III LG224 to Cairo via Gibraltar, arriving at Kabrit where they left the Wellington and joined 148 Squadron flying worn out Mk IAs. The busy airfield was shared with 40, 70, 104, and 108 Squadrons, and Hunter's crew were sent to Kilo 40 on the Cairo–Alexandria road. When the Battle of El Alamein started on 23 October 1942, a move was made to LG 106 at El Daba to provide support for the Eighth Army. The task was close support duties against enemy supply routes, each sortie taking up to three hours, but they had to fly two in one night to qualify for one operation.

Just prior to El Alamein, most of the operations were to Tobruk and Benghazi bombing shipping targets in the ports. The next move was to LG67 on top of an escarpment 30 miles south of Bardia, which was a challenge for the ground crews to deliver fuel and water bowsers up the slope. The Hunter crew made their last operation in the desert from El Adem to the Crete airfield of Casteli Peliadi. The squadron was disbanded on 31 December 1942, the remaining aircraft being left with 40 Squadron.

Led by Doug Skinner, a crew trained at 77 OTU at Qastina in Palestine were ready to join 104 Squadron. Their first operation was 17 November 1944 in a raid against troop concentrations and transports at Novi Pazar, but they were recalled to base before attacking. Returning the next day in daylight, they dropped three sticks of 250 pounders on enemy vehicles, followed by many more sorties against troop concentrations and transports, until Christmas Eve, when there was a general stand-down, except for unfortunate crews who drew straws for Christmas Day operations. One of straws was drawn by Doug's crew, which turned out to be a supply drop, making a return, exhausted, for a late Christmas dinner.

In the new year were more bombing and supply drops, when the weather became very cold, causing a drop to be aborted due to heavy icing on the wing leading edges at 11,000 feet. On 20 January 1945, the crew dropped their first 4,000-lb cookie from 8,500 feet on Odine marshalling yards with some light flak on the approach. The crew then were granted well-earned leave in Sorrento where they experienced the civilised luxury of running water and clean bed sheets. They returned to operations on 8 February when Verona was the target, followed by an oil refinery and harbour installations at Fiume on 15 February. On 20 February, the crew dropped their second cookie on Udine marshalling yards with the last trip on 24 February to Brescia marshalling yards, after which they were tour expired.

Complementing the desert bombing was also the disruption of supplies, including fuel and ammunition for the *Afrika Korps* from Italy. Malta was ideally placed as a base for Wellingtons adapted to firing torpedoes, but suffered heavy bombing, making the island almost untenable and challenging to defend from Axis attacks.

In 1941, the main anti-shipping capability was the Bristol Beauforts operated by 69 Squadron from Malta, later joined by 39 Squadron. The Beaufort could only carry a single 18-inch torpedo, and it was realised that an aircraft with a greater load carrying capacity and increased range was required to counter the threat. In December 1941, trials commenced at the Torpedo Development Unit based at Gosport in Hampshire with a Wellington Mk IC modified to carry two 19-inch Mk XII torpedoes enclosed within the bomb bay. On initial trials, the results were disappointing as the torpedoes regularly dived to the seabed when released. It was realised that the horizontal triangular tail surfaces for stabilising the torpedo in the air were not releasing on entry to the water. A hinged tail was fitted, solving the problem with trials restarting in March 1942; later in the year, they were cleared to release both in a stick, creating an improved chance of destroying the target ship.

In January 1942, 38 Squadron, as part of 201 Group, based at Shallufa, began training in the new anti-shipping role, using both a pair of torpedoes and also mine-laying against Rommel's supply convoys. This continued until the end of the year when the target area changed to Italian coastal waters and shipping off the Balkans. Torpedo strike squadrons were known as 'Fishingtons', operating Mk ICs and later Mk VIIIs, with 38 Squadron crews already familiar with low level night flying over the sea, who were naturally assigned to the task. The aircraft were modified, the front turret being removed and replaced by a rounded fairing, which must have been some concern for the crew when approaching well-defended shipping targets.

The usual bomb carriers were replaced by a pair of booms to carry two torpedoes. To ensure the torpedo hit the water in the right attitude, wood and canvas aerofoils were attached to the rudder and elevators of the torpedo, which broke away on entry into the water. To accommodate these aerofoils, there was as 'V' cut-out at the rear of the bomb doors, which allowed the torpedoes to be carried in the bomb bay, keeping drag to the minimum. The pilot used a sight located above the aircraft nose, consisting of a curved tube with small electric lamps fitted at intervals. The bulbs were painted black on the side facing the target to avoid showing the approaching target, and practice drops were made in Suez Bay against HMW *Sagittarius* and HMS *Roberts* as targets. In practice, this device was rarely used; the preferred method was flying low over the water, aiming the nose of the aircraft at the centre of the target ship, and releasing one or two torpedoes as near as possible to the target. The best way for departure was to lift up over the ship and drop down the other side at low level followed by a steep turn away.

When a convoy was detected, an ASV Wellington, or Liberator, would shadow it and transmit a homing signal for the torpedo Wellington to pick-up. Usually, half

No. 38 Squadron Wellington being loaded with a pair of torpedoes at Luqa, Malta. (*BAE Systems*)

Preparation of a torpedo for loading in a 38 Squadron Wellington at Shallufa, Egypt, during 1942. (*BAE Systems*)

Wellington bomb load including a line of incendiary bomb containers on starboard side. (*BAE Systems*)

the squadron carried a pair of 1,000-lb bombs and the other half two torpedoes. The bombing aircraft would attempt to distract any ships defences, while the Fishington would line the target up using any available moonlight and make its attack while the flak was hopefully distracted.

The first combat operation was attempted during the night of 22–23 February 1942 against a Tripoli approaching convoy with six bomb-carrying Wellingtons, accompanied by two Fishingtons, but only one of the bombers located the target and the torpedoes were carried back to base. Following a number of aborted operations, a second attempt was made on the night of 9–10 March, when Z9099 being flown by Wg Cdr Chaplin DFC was attacked by two Bf 109s, resulting in serious damage and a crash landing in the desert. The co-pilot and navigator were killed and the surviving members of the crew were rescued by members of the 4th Indian Division who returned them to Allied lines.

The first actual torpedo attack was against enemy shipping off Patras port, where the main target was an 8,000-ton cargo ship. In the initial attack, a torpedo was dropped at 1,000 yards range, but no results were observed. On a second attack in Z8983, a torpedo was released at 500-yard range, resulting in a hit just aft of the smoke stack causing a large explosion. Observations in the area an hour after the attack failed to locate the ship, making it uncertain if it had been sunk, or not.

More success was gained by 38 Squadron when they were equipped with Wellington Mk VIIIs, which were fitted with ASV Mk I radar. The four pole type radar aerials fitted on the upper fuselage caused the type to be referred to a 'Stickleback', and because of their role was also known as 'Goofingtons'.

The use of ASV radar had been developed by 221 Squadron at Bircham Newton in January 1941 using a modified Mk IC. The squadron deployed to the Middle East in January 1942 with sixteen 'Sticklebacks' to Luqa via Gibraltar, initially painted overall in white, but as they made easy targets, they were repainted in night bomber camouflage. They were initially based at LG 39 at Burgh el Arab South, south-west of Alexandria, supported by 47 Squadron ground crew while their own were travelling by sea from Liverpool. By February, they were flying on intensive anti-shipping operations, the first success being against an enemy convoy. Both 221 and 38 Squadrons often operated together, with the ASV-equipped aircraft identifying the target and passing information to the torpedo force, the ASV aircraft illuminating the target if necessary. By January 1943, both squadrons were equipped with Fishingtons and Goofingtons.

Early operations were lacking in success as although targets were located and reported, night torpedo attacks were poorly developed with no satisfactory operations. With plans gradually evolving and tested, encouraging results began to be achieved against Rommel's main bulk supply routes. Major problems were with serviceability, sand, and dust were hard on the engines. Only up to seventy flying hours were being achieved before an engine required changing. Aircrews were taking as many as six 4-gallon cans of oil to keep the auxiliary oil tank topped up. It required often up to 3 gallons per hour hand-pumped at ninety

Pegasus XVIII-powered Wellington GR VIII T2977 from 221 Squadron. (*BAE Systems*)

Wellington GR VIII DF-B from 221 Squadron 'stickle back' aerials. (*BAE Systems*)

strokes per gallon, giving 6 gallons per hour throughout a nine-to-ten-hour sortie. There were also problems with sticking valves, but once back on the ground, they appeared to disappear, making fault tracing by the ground crew difficult.

During the month before the Battle of El Alamein, Wellingtons were very busy with joint efforts by all anti-shipping squadrons interfering successfully with German seaborne supplies. This effectively stopped supplies of fuel, ensuring that by the time the Allied 8th Army defeated the *Afrika Korps*, there was no fuel remaining for the enemy to fight or retreat.

A typical combined operation took place on the night of 25–26 May 1942 when the target was an enemy convoy north-west of Benghazi by two torpedo carriers from 38 Squadron. The convoy had been located by an ASV aircraft and a Wellington set course, constantly checking the convoy position. The convoy consisting of two destroyers and two motor vessels was sighted, the MVs being around 8,000–10,000 tons and 2,000–3,000 tons. The larger ship was targeted with an approach from behind one of the destroyers, which opened fire on the Wellington, causing some damage. As the aircraft came around to approach the ship, smokescreens were developing as the crew fired their torpedoes. Although accurate observation was difficult due to flak and smoke, the ASV aircraft reported clouds of smoke billowing from the ship. During a reconnaissance the next day, a large cargo ship was spotted beached 30 miles north of Benghazi with a hole in the side. The Wellington had sustained some heavy damage to the starboard wing and fuselage, as well as the port engine, but succeeded in reaching LG 05 safely. The pilot, Sgt Youens, was awarded the DFM for the action.

On 21 August, a surfaced submarine was attacked by a Wellington escorting HMS *Coventry*, which was defending an Allied convoy. The attack was made at 20 feet with six depth charges dropped, one hitting the deck of the submarine just aft of the conning tower, and the remainder falling on either side of the stern. The stern was blown out of the water and the submarine submerged, but soon resurfaced, firing at the aircraft with its deck guns. These guns were silenced by the Wellington gunners, with the circling submarine until it sunk below the waves.

In late August 1942, Rommel started his final bid to defeat the 8th Army in North Africa and take over the Egyptian Delta zone. This required a considerable amount of supplies to be shipped to Tobruk, bringing Axis shipping well within range of the Wimpy torpedo strike aircraft based in Egypt. One of these convoys was located on 28 August steaming west of Crete, with a heavy destroyer escort. That evening, a combined force of Wellingtons and Liberators made an attack north of Derna, destroying one of the two main fuel-carrying tankers.

In the early hours of the next day, a second wave of Wimpy torpedo aircraft made a second attack. The targets were sighted in clear moonlight with a ship of about 8,000 tons protected by three destroyers, and Flt Lt Foulis of 221 Squadron flew around for about twenty minutes to determine the best method of attack. A low run was then started towards the ship's bow from the starboard side, where the ship was clearly visible. The first of two torpedoes was dropped at 400 yards while being fired on by one of the destroyers. With torpedoes on their way, both the target ship and destroyer opened fire at point blank range and the aircraft pulled up over the ship. Taking violent evasive action avoided any damage to the Wimpy, the navigator in the astrodome reported two bright explosions in the stern and midships. On circling the ship there was heavy smoke pall and a smell of burning oil. The first target report was sent, claiming two hits on the tanker, which was stationary. After about ten minutes when the smoke had cleared, there was only a large oil patch with the tanker obviously sunk.

By mid-1943, the most active part of the war in the Mediterranean was over with reduced targets for 221 Squadron torpedo attacks. Following the Allied invasion of Italy in September 1943, the squadron was used more for anti-submarine night patrols, in addition to up to twelve-hour convoy patrols. One of the tedious tasks for a member of the crew was to pump oil from a fuselage tank into both engines every hour. A co-pilot was often taken on sorties to allow the captain to have some rest during the long duration. Many of the co-pilots had not been trained on Wellingtons, so they may have had difficulty landing if the captain was disabled. These aircraft were Hercules-powered instead of the earlier Pegasus engines, giving an improved single engine performance. In addition to maritime operations, 221 Squadron was used occasionally for night bombing missions, illuminating targets that were usually communications arteries such as roads, railways, and bridges along the Italian coast, often at around 1,000 feet.

On 25 October 1942, a convoy of two freighters, four destroyers, and an escort ship was targeted between Malta and Tobruk. The 38 Squadron Wellingtons were attacked by three Ju 88s for fifteen minutes, but the slow speed of the Wellingtons with flaps and undercarriage down allowed them to escape.

Bombing and coastal strike were not the only duties of the multi-role Wellingtons in the Mediterranean Theatre. In the Mediterranean, 109 Squadron pioneered radio jamming with six specially modified Wellingtons fitted with additional fuel tanks and tropical filters on the engines. The squadron had originally been tasked with new equipment trials at Boscombe Down in December 1940, including Obeo. In October 1941, the crews were instructed to prepare for deployment to the Mediterranean to conduct trials on transmitters modified by Marconi and Ekco, to jam enemy tank VHF communications, with the anticipated German offensive in North Africa.

Squadron personnel were tasked with designing, manufacturing, and fitting the modified equipment and three aircraft departed for Egypt on 18 October 1941, known locally as Special Flight, but officially designated 109 Squadron Detachment Middle East, under the command of Wg Cdr W. B. S. Simpson. The initial operational flight was made from an advanced landing ground on 20 November, and subsequently captured enemy troops confirmed that radio jamming had caused disruption of tank communications.

The next day on a similar sortie, one Wellington was shot down by three Italian MC 202 fighters, one of which was claimed by another Wellington. Following continued operations, an interim report was issued, suggesting that the results

Wellington GR XIII MF419 from 221 Squadron in Italy 1944 with crew. (*RAF Museum*)

Wellington B X MF269 from 221 Squadron over Italy in March 1945. (*RAF Museum*)

achieved did not justify the resources deployed. There was no evidence that there had been any major disruption of enemy tank communications, and as there was no special effort to destroy the Wellingtons, it was obvious they were not a serious cause of disruption. It was considered a hazardous task for the crews to fly over the battlefield during daylight, and it was fortunate more were not shot down by anti-aircraft defences.

Despite this negative report, jamming operations continued throughout 1942, and the final report issued in December showed the army were unconvinced of the effectiveness of the jamming, known as Operation Jostle. Requests had been made to undertake jamming at night to avoid the hazards of daytime operations. Despite the perceived vulnerability, only one other Wellington was lost on the Jostle operations on 22 November 1941, also to an Italian fighter, with the loss of all six crew. Six sets of Jostle equipment were removed from the Wellingtons and stored in case of use in Beaufighters, which was considered a safer aircraft for the role.

A further specialised role for the Wellingtons in North Africa was active night reconnaissance by 69 Squadron, which was formed at Luqa in May 1942 with a variety of aircraft including Wellington Mk ICs and VIIIs. The target areas were enemy ports and airfields covering an area bounded by Libya, Sicily, and Italy. The Wellingtons were used for shipping strikes with bombs and torpedoes, in addition to flares for illuminating targets. Similar to the other Wellington bomber and torpedo squadrons, 69 Squadron Wellingtons attacked anything afloat, particularly tankers carrying fuel for the *Afrika Korps*.

By August 1942, the situation in Malta had become critical for supplies—both food for the population and in defence of the island—which had suffered so much from continuous Italian and German attacks. Operation Pedestal was conceived as a last-ditch attempt to rescue the island from enemy invasion, bringing much-needed supplies, including fuel from Britain via Gibraltar. The Wellingtons of 69 Squadron were tasked with night patrols around the coastlines of Tunisia and Sicily covering the convoy from hostile enemy aircraft and naval warships, especially when rounding Cape Bon, where it was attacked by many torpedo bombers and E-boats. The decimated convoy was able to reach Malta, breaking the blockade. Difficulties of operations from Malta resulted in rarely more than three Wellingtons being available, and when possible, the aircraft operating in pairs, one dropping parachute flares to illuminate the target, while the torpedo-armed Wellington would approach from the dark side, from where they were expected, at 50 feet and launch their torpedoes.

With Rommel's retreat following the decisive battle of El Alamein during October and November 1942, all six Wellington squadrons bombed enemy armour concentrations from desert landing grounds until the progress of the Allied advance allowed the use of captured enemy air bases in Libya, before taking up more permanent airfields in Tunisia and Algeria by February 1943. The Allied ground campaign was complemented by Operation Torch, the invasion of French North Africa in December, resulting in the Axis forces surrendering on 13 May

1943, allowing the RAF to turn its full attention to supporting the Allied invasion of southern Europe.

With new bases in French North Africa becoming established, the busy 205 Group Wellington squadrons were re-enforced by a number of Bomber Command units becoming available with the entry into service of the four engine heavy bombers in Britain. Among these units were 142, 150, 420 (RCAF), 424 (RCAF), and 425 (RCAF) Squadrons operating the new Wellington Mk Xs powered by improved Hercules XVI engines. This increase in size of the bomber force required the formation of local OTUs to provide replacement crews, and as already covered, 75–78 OTUs were established between December 1942 and January 1944, with 75 OTU being based in Egypt and the other three in Palestine.

On 1 January 1943, Blida-based 142 Squadron was tasked with bombing dock installations at Bizerte in Tunisia. One of the Wellingtons was loaded with a 4,000-lb cookie, which had a minimum height for dropping of 6,000 feet and the

The 1,675-hp Hercules-powered Wellington B X HE627 over North Africa. (*RAF Museum*)

Atlas Mountains only 20 miles inland. In an effort to get above the cloud, a climb was made to 13,000 feet, but it was still surrounded by cloud in violent turbulence. At this stage, the aircraft began to ice up rapidly, making flying challenging and unable to climb above the cloud, with the added weight of ice and loss of speed. With the target estimated to be 20 miles to starboard, a shallow descent was started aiming for searchlights seen in cloud. In the centre of the searchlight ring, the bomb was released, allowing the lighter aircraft to climb and emerge from cloud at 14,000 feet. The ice began to break off the airframe in large chunks, and a course was set for base, with a good astro-fix. At the Maison Blanche beacon, a rapid descent was started through cloud with the aircraft icing up again until 1,500 feet when warmer air cleared the airframe. With much relief, after six hours and fifteen minutes in the air, a safe landing was made back at Blida.

The 150 Squadron detachment was based at Blida, close to the Atlas Mountain inland from Algiers. Doug Newham was one of the navigators and found living conditions fairly basic, but they were able to trade with local Arabs to obtain a primus stove for cooking, and packing cases were used to make rudimentary beds and tables. The detachment continued bombing operations during the winter of 1942–1943 against enemy targets in Tunisia, Sardinia, and Sicily. On a raid to Ferryville, the bomb aimer scored a direct hit with a 4,000-lb Blockbuster on the lock gates. A number of crews were lost to enemy action, bad weather, and accidents, but the overall loss rate was significantly less than bombing operations over Europe at the time.

Doug considered to have been lucky to be posted to the North African campaign, as out of thirty-nine navigators who were trained with him at Jurby, he was one of only three to have survived—a staggering 92 per cent loss rate. Doug flew a total of thirty operational sorties on Wellingtons with 150 Squadron and returned to Britain by troopship in early 1943, when he was posted to 10 OTU at Abingdon to instruct navigators in the final stages of training. The only other flight in a Wimpy by Doug was with 10 OTU when he flew in a T Mk X on 18 July 1944 for 2.15 hours on local circuits and landings with Fg Off. Griffin. Doug then joined 10 Squadron in November 1944 operating Halifaxes.

Allied forces built up one of the largest RAF concentrations in Tunisia, consisting of three airfields at Kairouan inland from Sousse, including 70 Squadron, where living and operating conditions were much improved. Problems were caused by a couple of heavy rainstorms that turned the airfield surface into a quagmire, making it impossible to taxi, causing operations to be cancelled. The principal targets were in support of Allied ground forces advancing through Italy, German troop concentrations, and supply routes taking priority, in addition to the towns of Naples, Salerno, Taranto, and Turin.

On the night of 1–2 March 1943, thirteen 70 Squadron Wellingtons successfully bombed Palermo, and on 24 November, Turin ball-bearing works was the target. The Turin target was flown in terrible weather with snow, rain, and icy conditions. Once the target was reached, it was obscured by cloud, and bombs were not dropped until a busy road was spotted, where the load was dumped. A total of fifteen Wellingtons failed to return, five from 70 Squadron, due to intensive flak.

The Allied invasion of Italy commenced with Operation Husky, the landings on Sicily, and by mid-August, the whole of the island had been occupied, despite stiff enemy opposition from the beaches around the Strait of Messina, where 205 Group Wellingtons provided support. One of the 425 (RCAF) Wellingtons, HE978, gained the unequalled record for flying all of the squadron's thirty-two operations during the campaign against Sicily, the result being largely due to the hard work and dedication of the ground crew. On 25 August, Wellingtons of 70 Squadron began dropping 4,000-lb cookies, the target being railway marshalling yards at Taranto. By late October, Allied armies had crossed to the Italian mainland and advanced up the east coast, capturing the Foggia plain, where they were located at some existing enemy airfields. USAAF and RAF airfield construction battalions moved in to create additional temporary airfields laying PSP runways, taxiways, and hard standings, allowing 205 Group squadrons to move in. This brought Allied bomber forces within range of the entire German-occupied Europe, either from Italy or Britain, which created a major turning point in the war.

There were five RAF wings in 205 Group, and 236 Wing, as part of the group, moved from North Africa after the invasion of Italy to airfields on the Foggia plain. No. 236 Wing consisting of 40 and 104 Squadrons, both moved to Foggia Main on 30 December 1943 with Wellington Mk Xs, which they retained until March 1945, when replaced by Liberators. No. 205 Group complemented Bomber Command operations from Britain, but were in a smaller scale. Between February 1944 and April 1945, an average of sixty-three aircraft per night were despatched on bombing raids during 283 out of a possible 430 nights, but 215 aircraft were lost on combat operations.

Bomber crews in the Italian campaign did not have the advantage of the navigation aids available to Bomber Command in Britain; all flying was done by map-reading, dead reckoning, drift sights, and astro-navigation, sometimes with the help of radio direction finding (DF). In the first half of April 1944, 104 Squadron targeted the Macchi factory, railway installations at Leghorn, harbour facilities at Porto San Stefano, the airfield at Tokol, and railways and industrial facilities in Bucharest among other strategic targets. On 8 April, both 40 and 104 Squadrons joined 15th Air Force in support of Marshal Tito Partisans, who were surrounded by a large German force in the town of Nikšić in the Yugoslav mountains.

On 17–18 April, both 40 and 104 Squadrons were briefed for a raid on the major transport hub at Plovdiv in south Bulgaria, together with two squadrons from another wing. As the bombers taxied for take-off at 8 p.m., the first five 104 Squadron Wellingtons took off. They were followed by a 40 Squadron aircraft, but it crashed on take-off, hitting and setting two more Wellingtons on fire. The air and ground crews realised that the burning aircraft had carried a 4,000-lb cookie that could explode at any moment and took cover. The operation was cancelled that night.

No. 205 Group were busy on the night of 19–20 April 1944 with eighty-three aircraft sent off to a variety of targets, including a six-hour round trip to the port

Wellington B II W5584 after crash landing at desert airfield. (*BAE Systems*)

Wellington B IC X9693. (*BAE Systems*)

of Piombino in Tuscany opposite the island of Elba. No. 104 Squadron contributed twelve Wellingtons, a typical load being six 500-lb bombs and four 250-lb bombs. Weather and visibility were clear to the target for the first two waves, but cloud cover rolled in for the third wave, which bombed by dead reckoning. Despite heavy and light flak, there were no losses. The port and marshalling yards at Piombino were the target for the night of 21–22 April, and thirteen Wellingtons were allocated from Foggia Main, but after three had taken off, the next two both suffered burst tyres during take-off and crashed, luckily without casualties. Although the first managed to exit the runway, the second was unable as it was wrecked in the middle, preventing further departures. The three aircraft that did get away dropped their bombs on the target in hazy conditions and diverted to an alternate airfield while the runway was cleared of debris.

On the night of 4–5 May, seventy aircraft were allocated from 205 Group, including eight from 104 Squadron, the target being the Rakos railway marshalling yard at Budapest. The Wellingtons began departures from Foggia Main at 9.40 p.m. on what was expected to be a six-hour round trip. The target was marked by 614 Squadron Halifaxes, but flares were released late and became scattered. Flak was moderate and inaccurate, and night fighters were seen in the area, with only one Wellington lost with the crew. Operations continued on 5–6 May in Romania, 6–7 May in Bucharest, and 7–8 May to a bridge in south-west Romania; on 9–10 May, five aircraft bombed Genoa in northern Italy.

Also on the night of 9–10 May, seven 104 Squadron aircraft were part of a twenty-four aircraft force, which targeted a store of hundreds of Hs 293 radio controlled anti-ship glide bombers reported by the French resistance. The Allies needed to capture one of these stand-off weapons, and the first wave was to breach the walls, and fifteen minutes later, a diversionary raid was to be made on a marshalling yard about 1 mile from the initial target.

Four squadrons were involved, including 40 and 104, with the target at the extreme range of the Wellingtons, which required a refuelling stop at Cagliari in Sardinia. Loaded with bombs and fuel, the first wave (including seven 104 Squadron Wellingtons) departed, but when crossing the French coast near Cannes, the weather deteriorated rapidly, threatening the carefully co-ordinated plan. Severe icing caused some of the aircraft to abandon the operation and return for home, while those that continued towards the target suffered navigation difficulties with the target obscured. The second diversionary wave arrived over the marshalling yards 15 minutes later where the weather was clear, and they were able to bomb successfully. With the walls not breached by the first wave, the resistance fighters were unable to gain access and abandoned the attempted entry without an example of the missile.

No. 104 Squadron was on operations for seven continuous nights against harbour facilities on Elba, marshalling yards and railway bridges in German occupied Italy, being given a break for one night before another attack on Portoferraio. This was followed by violent thunderstorms which flooded the runways and stopped operations for four nights. Communications continued to be targets throughout May with a combined operation by the 15th Air Force on 25–26 May where some 1,000 vehicles were believed to have been destroyed around Viterbo, 40 miles north of Rome.

Viterbo was again the target area on 26–27 May for eight aircraft from 104 Squadron, followed by the squadron sending ten aircraft to the same target the following night. The last operation during the month was on 30–31 May, when 104 Squadron sent nine Wellingtons to bomb a road through Subiaco, east of Rome. Both 40 and 104 Squadrons were active on disrupting enemy communications in the Italian campaign, supporting the advance of the Allies through the challenging conditions.

From the winter of 1943–44 and into the following spring, 205 Group had come under the direct command of the 15th USAAF—the only time the RAF was under the control of another country. With the wet winter weather, the airfields on the Foggia plain became waterlogged and increasingly muddy, making operations more difficult. Living accommodation was poor on these temporary airfields, and catering was inadequate, with no bacon and eggs after return from an operation, as was the custom in Bomber Command. The toilet and washing facilities were very basic, and there was no social life off base. The crews wore army khaki uniforms as no RAF blues were available, leaving them feeling abandoned and forgotten.

On 11 March 1944, 70 Squadron was part of a force bombing marshalling yards at Foggia, and although under full cloud cover, bombs were aimed at flak on the ground. The next day, it was the turn for the marshalling yards at Sofia, Bulgaria by 150 Squadron, with the target clearly identified and marked by flares by 614 (Pathfinder) Squadron, making for the first time the use of pathfinder techniques in southern Europe, allowing significant successful destruction of the target.

On 20–21 September, marshalling yards in Hungary were targeted, with the lead aircraft achieving direct hits destroying rolling stock. The results of the raid could still be seen burning over 100 miles away during the return to base. On 6–7 July, Feuersbrunn airfield in Austria was bombed by 104 Squadron, following America bombers being attacked by fighters the previous day, but the results were inconclusive after a very long flight. During this raid, there was a full moon and defending fighters were able to take-off, devastating the force of fifty-one Wellingtons, with seventeen missing. It was chaos over the target with inaccurate path finding and the hazard of mid-air collisions due to aircraft flying in all directions. One crew climbed across the mountains and overhead, Graz was hit by flak under the tail, pushing the aircraft into a vertical dive that stopped the engines. The captain called for the crew to prepare to abandon the aircraft, but managed to pull out at 330 mph, with the engines restarted.

Among strategic enemy targets that gained RAF attention was the last remaining source of fuel in the major Ploesti oilfields in Romania. The USAAF had made an attempt to bomb these heavily defended oilfields on 1 August 1943 with a force of long-range B-24 Liberators operating from North Africa. With

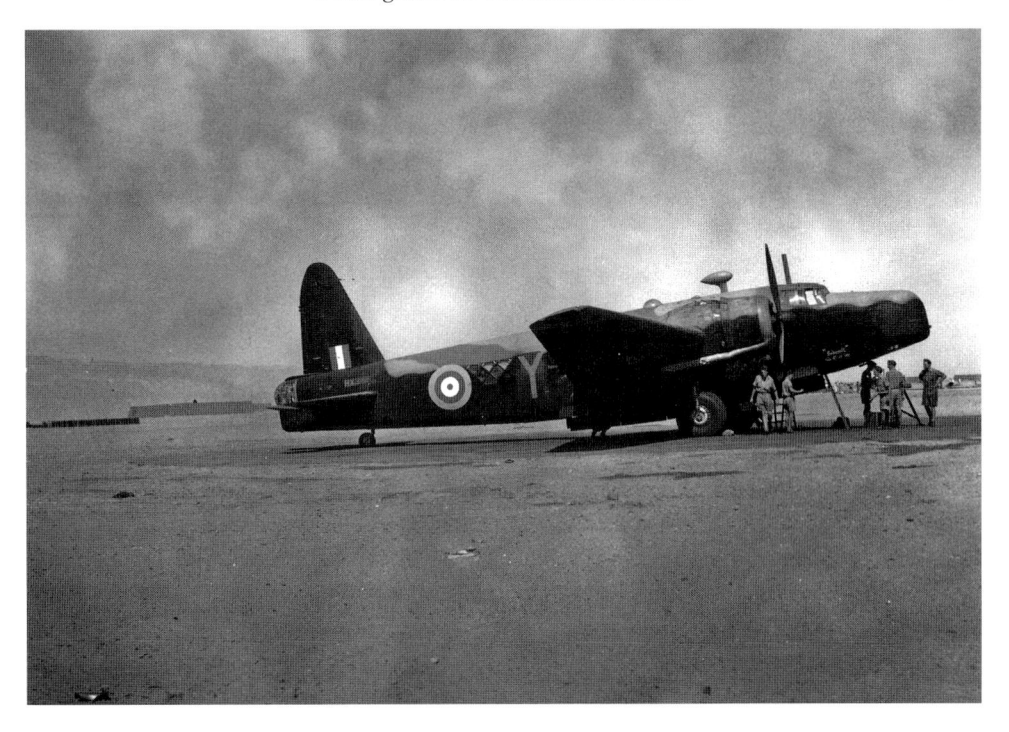

Wellington B X HE368 Y being prepared for next sortie. (*RAF Museum*)

Wellington B X LN317 with forty-five sorties and nose art. (*BAE Systems*)

the target now within the range of RAF medium bombers, repeated attacks were made to deny this fuel to the enemy. The anti-aircraft guns were located in the hills around the oilfields giving an umbrella defence, assisted by radar-controlled master searchlights, which when an aircraft was located by one, the others would home on to the bomber. There were also about 120 Bf 109s defending the target from the air, with another 200 monitoring the approaches from all directions. The force was led by Halifaxes and Liberators of 614 Squadron, who provided target marking, but attracted heavy flak. One of the RAF Wimpy units was Foggia Main-based 40 Squadron, with the bombing run being highly demanding.

Bombing altitude was between 12,000 and 15,000 feet, flying straight and level for the final thirty seconds on the bomb run, and after turning to fly towards Bucharest, the enemy was waiting with concentrated flak and night fighters. The bomber could be picked up by radar-directed searchlights within twenty-five seconds, but it was essential to maintain the approach to the target for successful bomb release. When a night fighter was detected approaching, the pilot was told to corkscrew towards the enemy in an effort to tighten the circle. Although the calibre of the Browning machine guns was not heavy, if they were concentrated to a point around 250 yards range, they could be very effective against Bf 109s and Ju 88s.

Wellington squadrons were ranging all over occupied southern Europe, with the bombing concentrating on enemy railway networks in Hungary and Romania, resulting in Germany making increase use of the River Danube, which ran 1,500 miles through Germany, Austria, Hungary, Yugoslavia, Romania, and Bulgaria, providing an artery for up to 10,000 tons of essential supplies daily. It was therefore vital to disrupt this supply line to enemy troops in south-east Europe, and 205 Group commenced mining operations from April 1944. Operations achieved a total of 192 mines laid on 1–2 July, dropped by a combined force of sixteen Liberators and fifteen Wellingtons. The main targets were freight barges, usually accompanied by heavily flak barges, reinforced by anti-aircraft guns located on hillsides and in cliff faces on narrow sections of the river, often firing down on the low flying Wellingtons. Due to low levels, casualties were high, as there was no possibility of abandoning the aircraft by parachute. In addition, the enemy strung cables from bank to bank in an attempt to snare the low-flying Wellingtons at often 50 feet above the river. Ideal conditions were a clear moonlight night, allowing identification of the target barges, a typical load being either two 1,000-lb mines or a pair of 2,000-lb mines. Approach to the target area was made at low level from the Yugoslav border to around Budapest, with a low-level return. The force was later credited with sinking 214 vessels.

During this campaign against targets in occupied Europe, there was still a need to neutralise targets in Germany itself, and 205 Group were tasked with these duties. On the night of 13–14 June, Munich was the target in the belief that a raid from the south would be a total surprise. However, the raid turned out to be a complete disaster. The first barrier was to flying 15,000 feet over the Swiss Alps, which was more than the height normally achievable by a fully loaded Wellington. A maximum climb rate was achieved after take-off, reaching 12,000 feet, which by careful coaxing slowly gained further height; some just managed to clear the top of the mountains. On arrival, there were no expected pathfinder markers, but the target area was illuminated by a path of searchlights about 30 miles long and 1 mile wide accompanied by heavy flak. As the bombers flew along the illuminated corridor, they were intercepted by around fifty fighters approaching head-on at about 1,000 feet above, but the enemy aircraft flew straight over the Wellingtons, apparently looking for the main stream of bombers. As it happened, there was no follow-up mainstream as 80 per cent were unable to gain enough height to fly over the Alps and aborted back to base. The few bombers that were able to cross the Alps were ineffective as the pathfinders had been shot down by the enemy, with the attacking aircraft releasing their bombs as soon as possible and turning for home.

By late summer in 1944, Wellingtons were operating to targets further into Hungary, Greece, Romania, and Yugoslavia, disrupting German communications by bombing airfields, railway viaducts, and marshalling yards. Marshalling yards at Miskole in Hungary were targeted on 22–23 August, but six Wellingtons were lost and others turned back due to bad weather. By this time, the aircraft were becoming worn out and unreliable, particularly the electrical systems. An important task in Yugoslavia was dropping supplies to partisan groups, who were doing their best to disrupt enemy activities, despite high risks.

The final pre-planned Wellington bombing raid of the war was on 13 March 1945, five and a half years after war started, when six 40 Squadron aircraft were part of a force of Liberators bombing marshalling yards at Treviso. Bombing appeared to be accurate with hits on the target area by 4,000-lb bombs, with all the crews returning safely to base. By this time, 40 Squadron was the last remaining Wellington unit in 205 Group, having delayed re-equipment with Liberators for this raid. Liberators re-equipped 37, 70, 104, and 148 Squadrons, while 150 Squadron returned to Britain to convert to Lancasters, and three RCAF Squadrons—420, 424, and 425—also returned to Britain to convert to Halifax. The surviving Wellingtons were struck off charge and scrapped during the spring of 1945.

6

Maritime Operations

In addition to anti-shipping and minesweeping operations in the Mediterranean, Wellingtons were adapted for anti-U-boat patrols with the use of air-to-surface vessel (ASV) radar, serving effectively in large numbers on maritime duties. The requirement was for detection in all weathers and at night by aircraft, of surface ships at the greatest possible range, but with a close in capability to bring the aircraft within visual range of the target. There was very little difference between the development of AI (airborne interception) radar to be used by RAF night fighters against enemy aircraft and ASV, both requiring the development of a light enough system to be carried in an aircraft.

On 17 August 1937, the first British airborne radar was flown in an Anson, proving it was possible to track Royal Navy capital ships in bad weather, but this was only an experimental version, with much further development required before service entry. Range was around 10 miles to detect a 1,000-ton ship, with up to 40 miles to spot land with significant sheer cliffs.

Introduced as ASV Mk I, some 200 sets were produced and installed in twenty-four Hudsons and twenty-five Sunderlands, but the equipment was unreliable; the manufacture quality was poor and it was challenging to maintain. ASV Mk I was not intended to detect submarines, but tests were carried out in late 1939 with a Hudson against a Royal Navy submarine, when it was found that flying at 1,000 feet, a submarine could be detected at 3 miles, broadside on. When flying at 6,000 feet the range was increased to 6 miles, but as it was an equipment test, the Hudson crew knew where to look. Long-range ASV (LRASV) was a sideways-looking system and was recognised by four pairs of dipoles located on the aircraft fuselage top and was first tested on a Whitley in late 1939.

ASV Mk II was developed by the RAE Farnborough and due to high standards of engineering was much more reliable. Range was up to 36 miles, with a minimum of around 1 mile, and several thousand sets were produced for installation in Hudsons, Wellingtons, Sunderlands, Beauforts, Warwicks, Whitleys, and Liberators, in addition to other Coastal Command aircraft. ASV Mk II was supplied in both forward-looking and sideways-looking LRASV, which was the only system capable of detecting submarines. The first success was by a Whitley on 30 November 1940 when *U-71* was damaged in the Bay of Biscay. By mid-1941, ASV-equipped aircraft had increased daytime attacks on U-boats by 20 per cent, and although night time attacks were possible, aircrew naturally had difficulty seeing a submarine, even only 1 mile from the target.

ASV development continued slowly due to priority being given to H2S ground-mapping radar, much to the dismay of Coastal Command. H2S was ineffective over the sea at altitudes flown by heavy bombers, with serious conflicts of interest between Bomber and Coastal Commands. The first Wellington unit in Coastal Command to be formed with anti-submarine Wellingtons was 221 Squadron on 21 November 1940 at Bircham Newton, equipped with rejected service aircraft for training and conversion. The first installation of Coastal Command ASV was made in a Wellington with a scanner fitted in the nose. Trials commenced with 221 Squadron in January 1941 using modified Mk ICs operating from Limavady from 2 May 1941, with detachments to Reykjavik in Iceland. On 15 May 1941, 221 Squadron Wellington W5671 was in action for the first time when an attack was made with depth charges well out in the Atlantic. The depth charges were dropped near the target, but not close enough to create any significant damage, although the action was good for squadron morale.

Wellington GR VIII W5671 DF-O from 221 Squadron at Reykjavik in 1941. This aircraft was used for shipping strikes, retaining the front gun turret and no Leigh Light. (*RAF Museum*)

Following this initial action, the squadron settled into a period of intensive flying with regular, low-level, nine–ten-hour sorties over the Atlantic, often in bad weather. On both 10 and 12 June 1941, survivors were sighted in lifeboats from torpedoed merchant ships and rescue ships were directed to the locations. On 2 May 1941, the squadron was detached to St Eval for better cover of the Bay of Biscay, and on 5 August, a U-boat was attacked by Wellington W5732. The U-boat was spotted on the surface, and following the attack, there was oil and some wreckage on the surface, with the submarine damaged enough to have to return to base for repairs. In January 1942, the squadron re-equipped with Wellington Mk VIIIs and was despatched to North Africa with detachments including Luqa in Malta.

On 1 March 1943, 172 Squadron operated the first patrol over the Bay of Biscay, and on 17 March, the first U-boat was located at night at 9 miles range, but the Leigh Light failed (see below); the first attack was therefore made the next day. By the end of the month, thirteen sightings had been made, and by May, Coastal Command had located and attacked the most U-boats in the Bay of Biscay. Sightings improving dramatically, and Allied shipping losses reducing from 400,000 to 100,000 tons per month. A total of fifty-six U-boats were sunk during April and May using a handful of aircraft fitted with ASV Mk III.

Wellingtons covered the vast area of the North Atlantic in search of U-boats threatening Allied convoys, at the same time reporting on icebergs and providing weather information. These patrols were not without risk as during the first year before moving to the Mediterranean, 221 Squadron lost seven aircraft with their crews from April to November 1941. Despite these losses due to accidents and combat, the squadron proved the concept of ASV, and the Wellington General Reconnaissance (GR) Mk VIII was produced by Vickers, fitted with the 'Stickleback' aerials along the top of the rear fuselage. The ASV Mk II fitted to these aircraft was developed by RAE Farnborough with an ideal range of 36 miles and could guide the Wimpy to within 1 mile of the target ship. These Wellingtons began to enter service during the spring of 1942.

The main task of Coastal Command Wellingtons was the destruction of U-boats during the Battle of the Atlantic, protecting the vital lifeline of supplies to Britain. This was also expanded to the protection of convoys passing through the Mediterranean. Twelve squadrons were re-equipped with the new type, mainly around Britain, but with two in the Middle East.

The first was 172 Squadron, which formed at Chivenor on 4 April 1942 from 1417 Flt, followed by the transfer of 304 (Polish) Squadron from Bomber Command at Lindholme on 19 July 1941 and 311 (Polish) Squadron from Bomber Command at Aldergrove on 28 April 1942. On 1 September 1942, 179 Squadron was formed at Skitten, moving to Gibraltar on 18 November 1942. On 22 October 1942, 547 Squadron was formed at Holmsley South, moving to Chivenor on 10 December.

In November 1942, 612 Squadron replaced Whitleys with Wellington Mk VIIIs at Wick, moving to Davidstow Moor on 18 April 1943 and then Chivenor on 25

Wellington GR XIV H-I from 172 Squadron at Chivenor in 1944. (*RAF Museum*)

Wellington GR VIII HX379 WN-A from 172 Squadron on patrol. (*RAF Museum*)

Factory-fresh Wellington GR VIII HX419 with a full array of aerials and powered by a pair of Pegasus XVIII engines, similar to the Bomber Command Mk IC. (*BAE Systems*)

May 1943. On 10 November 1942, 407 (RCAF) Squadron moved to Docking and replaced its Hudsons with Wellington Mk XIs in January 1943. Hampden-equipped 415 (RCAF) Squadron re-equipped at Thorney Island with Wellington Mk XIIIs in September 1943. On 7 April 1944, 524 Squadron reformed at Davidstow Moor with Mk XIIIs, moving to Docking on 1 July and Bircham Newton on 23 July. No. 14 Squadron moved to Chivenor on 24 October 1944 and exchanged Marauders for Wellington Mk XIVs and was disbanded on 25 May 1945 when it became based at Banff, equipped with Mosquito FB Mk VIs.

In the Middle East, 458 (RAAF) Squadron was re-established at Shallufa on 1 September 1942 with Mk ICs and Mk VIIIs, later receiving Mk XIIIs and Mk XIVs, disbanding at Gibraltar on 8 June 1945. In addition, 38 Squadron was transferred from bombing duties to the maritime role with torpedo-carrying Wellingtons as covered in the Mediterranean chapter. Other Wellington squadrons were formed for maritime duties in Africa and South East Asia, as covered later.

The major challenge for the crews was locating submarines at night, which had to surface in the dark to recharge their batteries. To overcome this, a powerful retractable searchlight was located under the rear fuselage. This was known as the Leigh Light and was a 24-inch diameter, 22-million candle-power unit, created by Sqn Ldr Humphrey de Verde Leigh, who was a staff member at Coastal Command headquarters. With the support of the C-in-C Coastal Command ACM Sir Frederick Bowhill, Wellington DWI P9223 was fitted with the first trial installation Leigh Light.

Wellington GR XIV MP774 from 179 Squadron with aircraft from 407 Squadron at Chivenor. (*BAE Systems*)

The 1,735-hp Hercules XVII-powered Wellington GR XIII JA144 ready for delivery to the RAF. (*BAE Systems*)

Hercules XVII-powered Wellington GR XIV MP818 with ASV Mk III in the nose and a Leigh Light under the fuselage, April 1944. This version was dedicated to anti-submarine work. (*BAE Systems*)

Initially power came from an auxiliary power plant, but later aircraft were fitted with battery packs. The light was fitted in a retractable ventral 'dustbin' in the fuselage underside, just to the rear of the wing-trailing edge, the designation of the Wellington being DWI Mk III, although it had nothing connecting it with the magnetic mine role, causing some confusion. Although Wellingtons had been equipped with ASV, in heavy sea states when a target had been detected, contact could be lost due to sea return on the radar screen, resulting in the Leigh Light being used to illuminate the target during the final approach to attack.

Early trials were successful, but adapting service aircraft was slow, as the Air Ministry preferred an alternative nose-mounted Turbinlite, which had been used unsuccessfully by Havocs in the night interception role. Leigh Light development was allowed to continue and was eventually adopted with 1417 (Leigh Light) Flt being formed at Chivenor on 8 January 1942 within 19 Group. The first four months were dedicated to intensive training, with the searchlight controls located in the aircraft nose so the light was swung back and forth, and up and down, until the target was illuminated.

Initially, only one Leigh Light Wellington was available for training, but more well-used Wellingtons were made available from Bomber Command to allow perfection of low-level bombing techniques. The training was not without its hazards as on a dummy night attack, what was thought to be a designated target ship turned out to be an American tanker steaming up the Bristol Channel. The alerted tanker crew opened fire, hitting the Wellington and killing the crew of a flight commander, the squadron's gunnery and navigation officers, and the normal crew complement.

No. 1417 Flt was equipped with four Wellington Mk VIIIs, with two reserves, and was under the command of Sqn Ldr Jeff Greswell. The first operational Wellington, W5733, was delivered on 8 February, followed by the first training aircraft, P9223, five days later, which had been used for trials. By the end of the month, it had been decided to bring the unit up to full squadron standard, when 172 Squadron formed on 4 April with a total of sixteen aircraft, plus four reserves.

By the summer of 1942, Leigh Light and ASV Wellingtons were patrolling over the Bay of Biscay, seeking out French-based U-boats going out or returning from North Atlantic convoy patrols. Once identified, the Wellington would illuminate and attack the submarine with depth charges, bombs, and gunfire. The light would be lowered by one of three wireless operators/air gunners 1 mile from the target at 250 feet using a radio altimeter, while a second wireless operator would direct the light onto the target using a short control stick. During final approach to the U-boat, altitude was reduced to 50 feet about 1 mile from the target, the precise height being measured by a radio altimeter.

When there was a significant swell, the radio altimeter indicator light varied from green to red if too low, and amber if above 55 feet. With the light lowered, the aircraft became longitudinally unstable. It was essential for the pilot to maintain control on instruments, as if he looked up, he was blinded by the light,

Wellington GR XIV with underwing RP, ASV, and Leigh Light. (*RAF Museum*)

lost orientation, and the unstable aircraft at 50 feet could crash into the sea. As a defence against Leigh Light attacks, U-boats could stay submerged at night and surface during the day, fighting the attacking Wellingtons with improved deck armament, while an air gunner fired the free-standing Browning guns. In the three-tiered bomb bay, four Torpex-filled depth charges, a long case of batteries for the searchlight, and an overload fuel tank were carried. Later, the batteries were moved into a wooden case in the nose under the searchlight operator's seat to improve the aircraft's centre of gravity. Powered by two Pegasus engines, the all-up weight was 33,000 lb, which meant in the event of an engine failure, there was little chance of maintaining height. Performance and load-carrying capacity improved when the Pegasus engines were replaced by 1,425-hp Hercules engines.

The first successful Leigh Light/ASV attack was during the night of 3–4 June by Wellington Mk VIII ES986 of Chivenor-based 172 Squadron, seriously damaging Italian submarine *Luigi Torelli*. Initial contact was made using the homing aerials at 6.5 miles to starboard, and as the target was approached, the Leigh Light was switched on, illuminating the submarine dead ahead. The aircraft was at 450 feet, and the target was obscured by the fuselage in the dive, resulting in the aircraft making another approach from 3.5 miles. For some reason, the U-boat sent up a couple of pyrotechnic signals that gave away its position, and it was illuminated at three-quarters of a mile. The Wellington descended to 50 feet and straddled the U-boat with four depth charges, three of which were seen to explode. The submarine was so badly damaged that it was unable to submerge and was attacked again by a Short Sunderland three nights later. It was forced to seek refuge in a neutral Spanish port.

Polish crews of 304 Squadron claimed two U-boats destroyed and a third badly damaged. The first confirmed sinking was on 18 June 1944 when Flt Lt J. Antoniewicz and crew sunk *U-441*, killing the entire crew. The submarine was returning to base at Brest at the end of a two-week patrol when located by the Wellington about 50 miles from port. The ASV radar in the Wellington was unserviceable, resulting in a visual attack in bright moonlight. As the U-boat was approached, another submarine was also seen, but continuing to *U-441*, which was beginning to submerge, six depth charges were dropped from 100 feet, straddling the target. There were violent explosions, resulting in wreckage and masses of bubbling oil being seen and no sign of the submarine. Meanwhile, the other submarine had submerged.

Leigh Light-equipped Wellington successes continued until the end of the war in Europe with the final U-boat sinking on 2 April 1945 by 304 (Silesian) Squadron, which sank *U-321*. During three years with Coastal Command, 304 Squadron made 2,451 combat sorties flying 21,331 operational hours. During this period, thirty-four U-boats were attacked and nine others were sighted. Of these, the Polish aircrews were able to claim just two U-boats destroyed and a third seriously damaged. The Wellingtons were intercepted thirty-one times by enemy fighters, losing 106 aircrew either killed or missing.

To increase Wellington effectiveness in maritime operations following the introduction of the GR Mk VIII, Hercules-powered GR Mk XI and GR Mk XII were produced, with the GR Mk XIV fitted with uprated engines. The most significant development for all these versions was the fitting of the much-improved ASV Mk III centimetric radar fitted under a nose-mounted chin radome. It provided a 60-degree field of view ahead and dispensed with the drag increasing stickleback aerials on the fuselage. In late 1942, the Germans had introduced the Metox radio receiver, which was able to detect ASV Mk II signals, resulting in much higher Allied shipping losses to the U-boat packs. The ASV Mk III had increased range and clearer resolution, and could be directed at the target more accurately.

The Torpedo Flying Unit (TFU) trialled the new radar in Wellington Mk VIII Z8902 in late March 1941. The first active use of the new equipment was on 1 March 1943 by 172 Squadron over the Bay of Biscay, and while on patrol on 17 March, they detected the first U-boat at a range of 9 miles. From then on, the rate of U-boat sightings increased dramatically. Admiral Karl Donitz, the commander of the U-boats, ordered his submarine commanders to stay surfaced and attempt to fight it out with attacking aircraft.

Following early successes in 1942, operations were increased as more squadrons were commissioned to attack U-boats. By March 1943, Operation Enclosure had been started by Coastal Command with greatly increased patrols over the Bay of Biscay allowing sightings on an average of once in every four sorties by 172 Squadron alone, with six sunk between March and July. The Wellingtons were armed with a variety of weapons, including depth charges against U-boats and a pair of torpedoes for other enemy shipping. In addition from late 1943, 612 Squadron Wellingtons could carry underwing-launched rocket projectiles, which could be very destructive both against surfaced submarines and shipping.

A typical crew consisted of six—the captain, second pilot, navigator, and three wireless operators/air gunners, the latter three manning the rear gun turret, radio, and radar. The radar operator was key to the operational success of the aircraft, and the three wireless operators/air gunners would take turns with the different duties. Each squadron had twelve aircraft allocated and would send out four or five aircraft individually each night, and with the other Chivenor-based squadrons resulted in ten aircraft patrolling the bay each night. Each patrol would take between nine and ten hours and there were few surface ships in the bay, apart from some Spanish fishing boats.

The Pegasus-powered Wellington Mk VIII replaced Beauforts in the anti-shipping torpedo role, and despite its increased size, it could be operated in a similar manner to the smaller aircraft. The robust structure allowed it to be manoeuvred effectively at low level. Training was carried out with the Torpedo Training Unit (TTU) at Abbotsinch from 19 March 1940 as part of 7 (Coastal) OTU and moved to Turnberry in November 1942, becoming 1 TTU on 1 January 1943. The crews were primarily being trained for night torpedo operations. Wellingtons could carry a pair of torpedoes and apart from the extra weight making take-off and

Hercules VI-powered torpedo bomber Wellington GR XI MP521 in January 1943. (*RAF Museum*)

Wellington GR XII MP512 in January 1943, which was operated by 172 and 432 Squadrons. (*RAF Museum*)

Wellington GR XIV with underwing RP, ASH, and Leigh Light. (*BAE Systems*)

Wellington GR XIV with full battery of RP under the wings. (*BAE Systems*)

general handling more demanding, the aircraft was stable when flying at low level over the sea.

Wellington crews were very successful against U-boats in the Bay of Biscay, patrolling as far south as Spanish territorial waters. Out of the 220 U-boats destroyed by Coastal Command, twenty-five were credited to Wellingtons, and significant contributions were made with many more sinkings. Almost a month after disabling the Italian submarine, 172 Squadron claimed its first victory when Plt Off. Wiley sunk *U-502* off La Rochelle on 5 July 1942 being awarded the DFC. The next day, Llandow-based Wellington BB503 flown by Flt Lt Southall sighted a U-boat at a distance of three-quarters of a mile in the Bay of Biscay. The attack was made from 100 feet dropping four depth charges set at 25 feet and spaced at 36 feet while the U-boat was still on the surface. All the depth charges exploded, straddling the U-boat's track just ahead of the bow. There was a sheet of flame from the explosion, and there was no further activity for two and a half hours. The assumption was the target had been sunk.

During the night of 22–23 December 1942, Chivenor-based Wellington LB150 was being flown by Fg Off. Stembridge at 1,600 feet when a contact was detected 6 miles ahead, which was seen as a dark object from 2 miles just off the starboard bow. By this time, the aircraft was at 700 feet making a diving turn to starboard, the pilot turning on the searchlight illuminating a surfaced U-boat. Continuing the diving turn down to 150 feet, four depth charges were released about 65 degrees to the target track. Although the U-boat had started to dive when illuminated, the conning tower was still visible when the weapons were dropped in a close circle at the centre of the swirl. The aircraft turned back on to a reciprocal course, but nothing further was seen. The same pilot was flying Wellington MP539 from Chivenor on 21 March and located a contact from 1,000 feet at a range of 7 miles. It was identified as a U-boat in the process of crash diving with the conning tower and stern still visible. The Wellington continued its dive and attacked at 60 degrees from port to starboard, dropping six depth charges from a height of 70 feet, causing a major explosion. On returning, two large patches of bubbles were seen, but there was no sign of the U-boat. It was later confirmed by the admiralty as the destruction of *U-665*.

Post-war research confirmed that *U-665* had in fact been sunk by Sgt Marsden flying a Whitley of 10 OTU, but it was concluded that Flt Lt Stembridge had actually attacked *U-488*, which was undamaged. He later sunk *U-437* on 28 April, being awarded the DFC, eventually rising to the rank of group captain, and received the AFC.

It was by no means a one-sided battle for the Wellington crews as the Bay of Biscay was also patrolled by Luftwaffe Ju 88s, which were successful in intercepting a number of RAF aircraft. A close call was during a 304 (Polish) Squadron daylight patrol by Wellington Mk IC from Dale on 4 February 1943. A silhouette was spotted by the front gunner 3 miles away to starboard, which was believed to be a ship. However, as they approached, it turned out to be a pair of Ju 88s, with the Wellington flying into the cover of cloud. On emerging, the enemy aircraft were seen over 15 miles away on a reciprocal course.

Surfaced U-boats were aggressive targets with heavy anti-aircraft guns on the decks. It was believed some twenty Wellingtons could have been shot down by U-boats, but many failed to return, without any knowledge of their fate. Some losses were identified from U-boat commander's logs after the war. *U-333* was caught on the surface in the Bay of Biscay by 172 Squadron Wellington MP50 on 4 March. The crew illuminated the submarine with the Leigh Light, and dropped four depth charges without causing damage. However, the U-boat's guns hit the Wellington, causing it to crash in flames into the sea.

On 8 September 1943, *U-402* was attacked by 172 Squadron Wellington MP791, which illuminated it with a Leigh Light and dropped six depth charges. Ten minutes later, another 172 Squadron Wellington also made an attack but was hit by anti-aircraft fire and crashed in flames in the sea with the loss of the crew, apart from one who was rescued by the crew of the undamaged U-boat. Later in the month, a 179 Squadron crew attacked *U-667* in Wellington MP722 but was hit by anti-aircraft fire while dropping depth charges; it was seen flying away with the Leigh Light still illuminated. Despite sending a SOS call, nothing further was heard from the crew. Wellington HF153 of 172 Squadron was hit by anti-aircraft fire from *U-764* during a strafing run on 27 November 1943; two of the survivors

Wellington GR XII MP684 with ASH Mk III centimetric radar and Leigh Light. The front gun turret was deleted, but in addition to the rear turret, there were side mounted 0.303-inch Browning guns. (*BAE Systems*)

were rescued by *U-238* and became POWs. The surviving wireless operator, Sgt Semple, was later able to convince the Germans that Allied aircraft were able to home passively on the radar detection systems, a deception which led to the order to turn off the Naxos radar when in combat.

U-boats also operated in the Mediterranean, and *U-343* was attacked by 36 Squadron Wellington HF245 on 8 January 1944. The five depth charges dropped missed their target, but anti-aircraft fire hit the port wing, which caught fire, resulting in the aircraft ditching. The pilot and navigator were killed, but the remainder of the crew were rescued the next day. *U-343* was then attacked again by two Wellingtons from 179 Squadron, with the second aircraft dropping six depth charges. Anti-aircraft fire set fire to the port wing, causing the aircraft to crash into the sea; only the pilot survived, being rescued the next day from his dinghy.

Back in the Bay of Biscay, *U-608* was attacked by 172 Squadron Wellington MP813 west of Bordeaux on 31 January 1944, but the aircraft was shot down with the loss of the crew and no damage to the U-boat. In February 1944, 612 Squadron Wellington MP758 was unable to attack *U-283* on the 10th due to heavy anti-aircraft defences, suffering engine trouble, and failed to return. The next day, 407 Squadron MP578 dropped depth charges on the same U-boat and succeeded in destroying it. On 24 May 1944, a 612 Squadron Wellington was shot down by *U-736* on the first operational sortie by the pilot, Fg Off. Davies, with all the crew lost. The entire crew from 192 Squadron was killed when flying HF449 was shot down by *U-618*, and on 14 August 1944, a 172 Squadron Wimpy was shot down by *U-445* in the Bay of Biscay.

On 27 August 1944, 172 Squadron Wellington NB798 was shot down by *U-534* despite dropping six depth charges, with the port engine stopped and the aircraft ditched. Two of the crew were able to get into a dinghy, with two more hanging on. The navigator died in the night; the survivors were rescued by a Sunderland. The navigator, Fg Off. Gray, was awarded the George Medal posthumously as despite his wounds, he refused to climb into the two-man dinghy in case he endangered the other survivors; Gray died in the water.

As some means of defence when attacking U-boats, the commanding officer at Chivenor arranged for forward-firing light machine guns to be fitted to Leigh Light-equipped 172 Squadron aircraft. The gun was not heavy enough to structurally damage a U-boat, but it was hoped it would keep the heads of the U-boat gunners down during a depth charge attack. After the initial success of Leigh Light-equipped Wellingtons, sinking of U-boats declined. From Chivenor three U-boats were later claimed destroyed, one by the RAF, another by a Canadian squadron, and the third by a Polish crew. The main task was to keep the U-boats below the surface.

No. 612 (County of Aberdeenshire) Squadron had replaced its Whitleys at Wick with Wellington Mk VIIIs in November 1942, which were replaced by Mk XIIIs in March 1943. A move was made to Davidstow Moor on 18 April, followed by a number of postings to Chivenor where Mk XIVs were added to the fleet. After a spell at Limavady, a return was made to Chivenor on 1 March 1944 to help provide support in the Bay of Biscay for the planned D-Day Allied landings. The Leigh Light Wimpys were fitted with the more sensitive ASV Mk 3a. Following D-Day, the squadron was posted to Limavady again on 9 September where the radar was effective in detecting the *Schnorchel* used by submerged U-boats operating in the Northwest Approaches between Scotland and Iceland.

On 19 December 1944, the squadron was moved to Langham where they took on the anti-shipping role covering the area from the Hook of Holland to the German coast to deter enemy convoys attempting to reinforce German armies in support of the Battle of the Bulge in the Ardennes Offensive. The radar was particularly effective as it released the bombs on the target, but the aircraft had to be flown at 1,250 feet to ensure accuracy was maintained. Support was often provided by rocket- and cannon-armed Beaufighters and Mosquitos, who would follow through the Wimpy attack with RP and 20-mm cannons. The squadron disbanded on 9 July 1945.

In November 1944, the crews of 14 Squadron had completed two years of operations in the Mediterranean flying Maurauders and were posted to Chivenor where four Wellington GR Mk XIVs were ready for them. With the intention of searching for U-boats, the Wimpys were fitted with Mk VI radars operated by an additional crew member. These aircraft were also fitted with a retractable Leigh Light in the belly, and flying was due to start on 30 November, but it was curtailed due to bad weather and poor serviceability of the aircraft. The anti-submarine patrols required a rigid crew discipline, with the pilot flying on instruments, the navigator maintaining position in the required area, and the radar operator searching for targets. Once a target was detected, the radar operator would take over and provide the pilot with directions ready for a Leigh Light-assisted attack. As part of the training, a Royal Navy minesweeper was positioned in the Bristol Channel to allow crews to carry out search and homing profiles. The first operational maritime sortie for 14 Squadron was during the night of 2–3 February 1945 on an anti-submarine detail in the St George's Channel, with the second sortie three nights later in high winds and over a rough sea. By March, the squadron was flying up to five operations a night.

Anti-submarine patrols were a demanding and unglamorous task, usually carried out at night and in bad weather. It required intense concentration flying on instruments for up to ten hours, which was exhausting not just for the pilot, but unrewarding and boring for the navigator, and the radar operator, having to concentrate on the screen, often ended up suffering from headaches. A near experience with combat was on 11 March when a crew with an unserviceable ASV sighted a US Navy Liberator on a parallel course some 8 miles away. The Liberator suddenly turned having sighted *U-681*, and the Wellington followed. The Liberator dropped depth charges sinking the submarine as the Wellington crew were preparing to provide back-up.

Combat was not the only hazard, as weather and fatigue played a significant part. On 18 April 1945, a crew led by Flt Lt Overed, flying NB858, took off at 9 p.m., heading for the Western Approaches. Four hours after take-off, a brief SOS message was received from the aircraft, but there was no further contact despite transmissions requesting further information. Another Wellington on patrol was diverted to the suspected search area, but found nothing, returning to Chivenor with minimum fuel remaining after being airborne for eleven hours. A few days later, the body of one of the crew was washed ashore near Bilbao in Northern Spain. On the same night, Flt Lt Hogg had taken off in NB875 before Overed, and just before midnight, he radioed that he had a fuel leak and planned to divert to St Eval in Cornwall. The aircraft located St Eval in clear weather, but on the approach to the airfield, it hit cliffs a few miles before the runway and all were lost in the fireball.

By this time, it was obvious that the European war was coming to an end, and on Victory Day on 8 May 1945, Flt Lt Walker was one of the crews airborne, qualifying for the distinction of having flown on both the first and last days of the war, having started at a Blenheim gunner in September 1939. With the flying activities winding down, Chivenor reverted to peacetime with the last operation of the war flown on 29 May by Flt Lt Gibbs in NB821 on convoy escort duties in the Irish Sea. Two days later, the squadron Wellingtons were grounded, although the squadron was officially disbanded on 25 May.

On 1 September 1944, 172 Squadron with Mk XIVs was moved from Chivenor to Limavady to cover the Northwest Approaches. However, by then many of the U-boats were capable of underwater breathing using a periscope, and such a small target in a rough sea was difficult to detect. Around this time, the first sonobuoys were introduced to detect U-boat noise when submerged. At the end of the war, the U-boats were ordered to surface in two lines—one in the Bay of Biscay and the other the Northwest Approaches. The Wellington crews were surprised to see so many U-boats, and they were escorted to Ballykelly, where they surrendered.

With the U-boat threat much reduced in the latter stages of the war, the new menace was from heavily armed E-boats and midget submarines operating in the southern part of the North Sea, threatening supplies for the advancing Allied armies. Based at Bircham Newton from 15 November 1943, 415 (RCAF) Squadron flew Wellington Mk XIIIs from a number of detached airfields on almost constant E-boat operations, but suffered radar jamming by the enemy.

Formed specifically on 7 April 1944 at Davidstow Moor to counter E-boats in the build up to D-Day was 524 Squadron equipped with Wellington Mk XIIIs. The first of eight experienced crews were posted to the squadron on 20 April ready for the initial operation on 30 April along the French coastline. This was to identify and illuminate enemy targets which were then usually attacked by Beaufighter strike aircraft, in addition to carrying out its own bombing sorties. The crew normally consisted of two pilots, a navigator and three wireless operators/air gunners who shared duties on the radar and rear gun turret. A combination of the radar and powerful flares were essential for target illumination of E-boats, which operated under the cover of darkness in all weathers.

During May, 524 Squadron crews started to work with the anti-shipping hard-hitting Beaufighters of 144 and 404 Squadrons also based at Davidstow Moor. With often difficult weather conditions, 524 Squadron aircraft were pre-positioning to the better-equipped Dunkeswell, where weather was often better, and had the advantage of being nearer the area of operations, allowing longer patrols. The Wimpys carried 250-lb or 500-lb medium-capacity bombs, which were fitted with air pistols set to detonate at about 100 feet above the surface of the sea to create maximum damage to the high-speed craft. E-boats usually operated in packs of between three and six travelled at up to 35 knots, whatever the sea state. During the first month of operation, the squadron flew forty mostly uneventful operations, but with the start of the invasion of Europe by the Allies, the tempo increased with 524 Squadron concentrating their efforts off Cherbourg and the Channel Islands.

Once the Allied landings were established and liberating France, the German threat reduced in western France, 524 Squadron moved to Docking in Norfolk on 1 July to begin patrols along the Dutch coast. It absorbed the Wellington Flight of 415 Squadron RCAF also based at Docking, doubling its fleet of Wellingtons to sixteen aircraft. On 7 July, the squadron began operations from its new base bombing ships in the Somme Estuary, however, losses commenced with MF375 shot down by flak on 9 July and MF374 failed to return from a raid on 13 July. With Docking remaining a forward base, 524 Squadron HQ and maintenance facilities moved to the better-equipped Bircham Newton on 23 July. Other advanced bases used were Manston and Thorney Island depending upon the area to be patrolled. Despite disruption caused by these moves, the squadron was able to operate eighty sorties in July, including attacks on enemy coastal shipping and escort vessels.

Targets were usually identified by radar in coastal area patrols some 60 to 80 miles in length at heights of 2,000 to 3,000 feet, depending upon weather and visibility. Priority was mostly reporting all contacts in the patrol area, with attacks were only permitted by permission from Group. On some occasions, attacks could be made at the captain's discretion, but only after reporting to Group. Bombs were usually dropped from 2,000 feet to avoid the shock of the explosion in the aircraft, but any results were usually hard to assess.

The squadron operated with North Coates-based Beaufighters of 455 and 489 Squadrons on Operation Purblind attacking enemy convoys, with 524 Squadron locating and illuminating targets for Beaufighters. On an attack against shipping off Cherbourg, a 524 Squadron Wellington laid a circle of markers about 15 miles from the target shortly before the Beaufighter's ETA. On instructions from the Beaufighter leader, the Wellington then laid flares behind the target shipping, highlighting it, allowing the Beaufighters to make an effective attack. The Wellingtons also operated individually, an example being on the night of 6–7 July when two out of eight E-boats were sunk, but losses continued on these hazardous missions with two aircraft lost on 1 September.

The rest of the month was successful with a dredger sunk in Scheldt estuary on the night of 11 September and with another crew in support on the same night a 2,500-ton T-61 torpedo boat was sunk by 143 Squadron Beaufighters and 855

Naval Air Squadron (NAS) Avengers off the West Frisian Islands. The following night, another enemy ship was sunk by the same combination in the same area. Wellington GR Mk XIII MF577 was one of four 524 Squadron aircraft supporting 489 Squadron and 855 NAS and although routine messages were received, all in clear weather, Flt Lt A. R. Brown and his crew failed to return to base.

With the approach of severe winter weather in northern Europe, 524 Squadron was fully committed, but due to Docking becoming waterlogged, a move was made to Langham on 17 October 1944. During December, the first Wellington GR Mk XIVs were delivered fitted with an improved centimetric ASV Mk III radar with operations continuing as crews converted to the newly equipped aircraft. In addition to flak, there was also a threat from night fighters, with Mk XIV HZ644 shot down by a Ju 88G on 14 January off the Frisian Islands with the loss of all the crew. On the night of 24 February 1945, an E-boat was sunk off Scheveningen by the crew of HF283, but the aircraft was also hit and forced to ditch with the fuselage on fire. Sadly, only the pilot, Flt Lt Davis, and his navigator were rescued. In the early hours of 6 March, three E-boats were located by the crew of NB772, leaving at least one damaged.

Wellington GR XIV NB802 with ASH, Leigh Light, and bomb doors open. (*BAE Systems*)

In April 1945, the squadron participated in Operations Taboo and Physic directing Royal Navy warships on to their targets with flares, which continued until its final action on the night of 25–26 April when four minesweepers were hit. The last sortie was on 11 May. The squadron disbanded on 25 May 1945, having lost ten aircraft during its brief career.

Already mentioned briefly, Mediterranean operations were generally similar to the Coastal Command waters around Britain. The protection of Allied convoys through the Straits of Gibraltar was shared between 179 Squadron, which was based in Gibraltar from 18 November 1942, and 36 Squadron, which arrived at Blida in Algeria on 24 June 1943, both equipped with Mk VIIIs. The eastern end of the Mediterranean was protected by 458 (RAAF) Squadron, which was initially based at Shallufa in Egypt from 1 September 1942 with Mk ICs and Mk VIIIs. There were detachments to Gambut, Berca, and Luqa, replacing the earlier aircraft with Mk XIIIs from June 1943. Both 38 and 221 Squadrons added to their previous successes against surface shipping and were also were involved in GR operations.

Much of the flying was for long periods of over ten hours at night, often with no success. No. 179 Squadron provided support for an American convoy with

The 1,735-hp Hercules-powered Wellington GR XIVs of 458 (RAAF) Squadron at Gibraltar in 1944 fitted with ASV Mk II for low-level patrols. (*BAE Systems*)

Wellingtons of 38 Squadron at Grottaglie in late 1944. (*BAE Systems*)

Malta-based Wellington GR XIVs of 38 Squadron over the Mediterranean in 1945. (*RAF Museum*)

supplies in support of the North African landings at Casablanca, and because of radio silence being observed, all signals were by Morse code using Aldis lamps. Although a blip on the ASV could be a surfaced U-boat, on investigation the result was often a fishing boat or Allied warship, which could be a hazardous from 'friendly fire'. All this chasing around kept the navigator busy to ensure the position was known resulting in a safe return to base. The short 900-yard runway at Gibraltar was challenging for some of the well-worn Wellingtons, carrying extra fuel and 1,000 lb of depth charges, the only saving grace sometimes being the 30-foot elevation of the end of the runway over the ocean, allowing a gradual climb away.

Some successes were claimed by 179 Squadron. One of the crews claimed three U-boats in quick succession in late 1943. The first was *U-431* on 21 October, then *U-566* on 24 October, and *U-542* on 26 November. Another crew sunk *U-134* on 21 August, *U-211* on 19 November, and *U-760* was so badly damaged that it went into the Spanish port of Vigo, where it was interned.

Although U-boats became harder to detect from 1944, there were other targets to attacks. A 38 Squadron crew located an Italian midget submarine on 3 April 1945 and sank it off Rimini. No. 36 Squadron was equipped with various Wellingtons fitted with ASV radar, Mk XIV HF272 making an attack on a U-boat during the night of 16 May. The Leigh Light might have assisted with location of the target, but the submarine anti-aircraft guns had an excellent illuminated target to aim at. The U-boat was damaged and attacked again by HF298 also of 36 Squadron, which forced the submarine to surface, allowing the crew to escape before it sunk. Enemy submarine losses became so high that no further U-boats entered the Mediterranean through the Straits of Gibraltar, where they could be easily detected.

As part of the Middle East Wellington maritime force, 621 Squadron was formed at Port Reitz, Kenya, on 12 September 1943 with Wellington XIIIs; the initial patrol area was the Red Sea moving to Mogadishu on 1 November and Khormaksar, Aden, on 5 December. The squadron operational area was vast and included the Persian Gulf. On the morning of 2 May 1944, 621 Squadron Wellington 'T' Tommy with a crew led by Flt Lt R. H. Mitchell was carrying out an anti-submarine patrol south of the Gulf of Aden. Much to their surprise, they spotted *U-852* steaming along at 12 knots on the surface. As the Wimpy turned in to attack, the U-boat commander gave the immediate order to crash dive, but it was too late. At a range of 600 yards, the front gunner opened up, and at 50 feet, a stick of six depth charges straddled the target. The damage was sufficient to prevent the submarine submerging and left it wallowing on the surface. Six further attacks were made during daylight hours by 621 and 8 Squadrons against spirited defence from the enemy gunners. HMS *Falmouth* was on convoy protection nearby and was sent to the scene, sighting the U-boat in the early hours of the next morning. To avoid capture of the submarine, the commander scuttled the damaged vessel, with the surviving crew members making for the nearby shore, where they surrendered to a naval landing party.

With the Allied planned landings at Nice, Wellingtons of 36 Squadron flew a mock invasion pattern off Marseilles in August 1944, with three Wellingtons dropping window (aluminium foil strips) over three landing craft 1 mile apart to confuse radars. As the Wellingtons flew over the landing craft, they turned through 180 degrees back, gradually closing to within half a mile from the coast, when they were fired on by enemy guns.

The increasing number of operations over the sea brought greater risk of crews being forced down in the water, or having to abandon their doomed aircraft by parachute. The loss of these experienced crews dying of exposure in their dinghies was unacceptable and needed to be dealt with effectively. The fleet of RAF rescue launches had been doubled in 1940, but dedicated search aircraft were required to cover a wider area and spot survivors from the air, although this was often difficult due to the small targets and poor weather conditions. From 1941, a number of dedicated rescue squadrons were formed in Britain, usually flying Ansons or Lysanders, carrying out searches of areas where survivors may be located around the relatively short ranges of the North Sea and English Channel.

The Mediterranean was more of a challenge due to its larger area requiring long range maritime rescue aircraft. An air-sea rescue and communications flight formed at Hal Far in Malta on 1 March 1943 using a number of different aircraft, including Wellingtons to conduct searches. When survivors were located, Westland Walrus amphibians were despatched to land alongside and recover the downed aircrew. In August, the flight moved to the neighbouring island of Takali, but returned to Hal Far in January 1944 to change role from rescue to communications.

Rescue aircraft based in Malta were only able to cover the middle of the Mediterranean, with the eastern and western ends covered by 1 (North Africa) Air-Sea Rescue Unit, based at Sidi Ahmed in Tunisia from June 1943, but was disbanded in December. During its short existence, it was initially equipped with four well-worn Wellington Mk ICs, but due to their unsuitability, they were replaced by a Mk X and a Mk XIII. The crews usually consisted of two pilots, a navigator, and three wireless operators/air gunners, all of whom were used as lookouts, as well as self-defence. Search duties could take over eight hours per sortie, often with no results, and some twenty-five operations made each month looking for crews from overdue Beaufighters, Hudsons, and B-17s. One rare success was the location of five crew members of a Marauder on 30 July who were rescued by a Catalina, although it was unable to take-off and a rescue launch eventually saved the survivors.

To take over rescue duties in a more formal way, 294 Squadron was formed at Berca near Benghazi on 24 September 1943 equipped with Walrus and Wellington Mk ICs. The Mk ICs were replaced by Mk XIs in March 1944 and Mk XIIIs in June 1944, with Warwick Is added in October 1944. The squadron disbanded on 8 April 1946 at Basra. The squadron was under the control of the Aircraft Safety Centre, Persian Gulf, with headquarters in Bahrain, the squadron moving to Amriya South in Egypt on 5 October 1943. No. 293 Squadron formed at Blida

The 1,735-hp Hercules-powered Wellington GR XIII JA640 ready for delivery. (*BAE Systems*)

No. 294 Squadron's Wellington GR XI MP640 at Idku, 1944–1945. (*RAF Museum*)

Wellington GR XIII from 294 Squadron at Idku in March 1945. (*RAF Museum*)

Wellington GR XIII JA412 S on patrol over the Mediterranean. (*BAE Systems*)

in Algeria on 28 November equipped with Warwicks, a Wellington development, to cover the western end of the Mediterranean.

No. 294 Squadron was kept busy although sadly not all their sorties were successful. During February 1944, a Beaufighter crew was found and saved on 25 February. They were also successful on 29 February when another Beaufighter crew was located during an eight-hour sortie. No trace was found of five crews. Although the overall rescue programme resulted in only a few survivors, many of those missing could have been killed in combat.

Maritime Wimpys were a significant defence against enemy submarines, sinking or seriously damaging at least fifty-one U-boats from 1942 until the end of the war. They also provided a major deterrent in the defence of Britain's vital merchant shipping convoys, bringing both commercial and military cargoes to the beleaguered country. Maritime patrols by all Allied aircraft required endless patience during monotonous flying over featureless oceans in all weather conditions, day and night. It was rare to find even a hint of a U-boat, and harder still to claim any success. It was a combination of stoic patience, mental and physical endurance, with the capability for instant and effective reaction when a target was located.

7

Asia, Africa, and Arabia

Front-line combat with Wellingtons around Europe and Mediterranean were the primary areas of operations, but the less publicised and often more arduous critical activities were in South East Asia in support of Lord Mountbatten of Burma against the Japanese.

With the Japanese attacks on Singapore in December 1941, the only bombing capability was a tactical one with four squadrons of Blenheims based in Malaya, which were ineffective against the massive enemy forces that captured Singapore on 15 February 1942. The offensive effort by Britain was the 14th Army, known as the 'Forgotten Army', at the most distant point from Britain with all the logistical challenges. The same applied to the RAF units based in the region.

Following the surrender of Singapore, enemy forces began a rapid advance into Burma heading for India and Middle Eastern oil fields. As a result, it was decided to send Wellington-equipped 99 and 215 Squadrons to India with support personnel and materials travelling by sea. The choice of 99 Squadron was natural as it had been gifted with a full complement of Wellingtons by the citizens of Madras becoming known as 99 (Madras Presidency) Squadron. The squadron had first equipped with Wellington Mk Is at Mildenhall in October 1938 and on 8 March 1941 was based at Waterbeach, receiving Mk IIs in July until October. It is recorded as being *en route* to India on 12 February 1942 and was re-established at Ambala on 1 June, moving to Pandeveswar on 12 September, ready to equip with Wellington Mk ICs in October. While flying six Wellingtons to India, the aircrews were delayed in North Africa with the task of doing some local ferrying work for the crews in theatre.

Operations with 99 Squadron started on 18 November with an attack on Meiktila airfield by eight Wellingtons from their new base at Digri, east of Calcutta, which was nearer to the intended operations. These operations were mostly at night over the Indian Ocean and jungles of Burma, later going north

A 99 Squadron Wellington wreck in India. (*BAE Systems*)

to Mandalay, with some of the sorties taking over ten hours. By the autumn of 1942, 99 Squadron was fully operational, and during a raid on Meiktila on 23–24 November, seven Wellingtons were attacked by a force of defending Nakajima Ki-43 Hayabusa fighters. Wellington DV875 was attacked with the rear gunner mortally wounded and severe damage to the aircraft. During a forced-landing at Chittagong, the aircraft burst into flames, killing one crew member. The pilot died the next day from his injuries.

During December, many Wellingtons with 99 Squadron were unserviceable due to engine problems, with three out of eight sent on a raid having to return. After investigation, it was found that the use of 100 octane fuel was causing valves to stick, and a change to 90 octane fuel solved the problem. Despite hard work by ground crews, serviceability of the Wellingtons suffered due to the hot humid climate and the poor supply of spares and ground equipment, resulting in only half the aircraft being available for combat during the initial months of the campaign. With the Bengal Maintenance Wing established in early 1943, support improved for the squadron ground crews and with more spare parts available.

Offensive operations were started in February 1943 when Brigadier Orde Wingate led the Chindits into Burmese territory well behind enemy lines as the long-range penetration group. Support was provided by the RAF, although the monsoons often led to operations being cancelled. During an attack on Heho airfield on 1–2 April 1943, a 99 Squadron Wellington was badly damaged and had to be abandoned by the crew, who were taken prisoner.

The strategic port city of Akyab was attacked by five Wellingtons of 99 Squadron on 7–8 September from Jessore, but the crews were unable to locate their target due to cloud cover in the target area. They returned to base with the bomb load, with one of aircraft suffering engine failure and ditching in the sea, killing two crew. The other three were able to take to the dinghy and were rescued by an air-sea rescue launch almost twenty-four hours after crashing.

During the final year of Wellington operations over Burma, serviceability had improved considerably, allowing a total of fourteen aircraft going on a raid at a time. The main targets were Japanese supply routes, with railway installations taking particular priority. An example was on the night of 18–19 January 1944 when marshalling yards at Mandalay were attacked. Wellington LN331 had the port engine fail an hour into the return journey, but by jettisoning everything possible from the aircraft, and having the good luck to find valleys to fly through, they were able to make a safe landing. If crews abandoned their aircraft over the dense jungle, there was little chance of survival as parachutes could be hung up in the trees. If they were able to reach the ground, it was rare to be able to walk out.

With Japanese occupying the whole of Burma at the beginning of 1944, there was a major attempt to break through to India. The priority for the RAF was to attack enemy strong points to delay the assault. On 25 April, a bold attempt was made using 4,000-lb cookies to cause a landslide to block the Tiddim to Imphal route, but it was impossible to see how successful the raid had been due to the vast cloud of dust thrown up. For several months, the crucial battle of Imphal required major support from Wellington squadrons.

By June, the Wellington units were used almost exclusively to bring bombs into the Hurricane Fighter Bomber airfields, where they could be used tactically to support ground forces. During the month of June, 99 Squadron flew 171 supply sorties, totalling 261 tons of bombs. The last Wellington loss with 99 Squadron was Mk X HZ719 when acting CO Sqn Ldr Ennis was shot down by Japanese fighters on 17 June 1944 with the loss of all six crew.

Wellington crews were able to return to bombing operations in July with improved situation on the ground, operating reconnaissance and offensive patrols with airfields and bridges targeted both day and night. The final Wellington operation in the theatre was by 99 Squadron on 15 August 1944 when eight aircraft made an accurate daylight raid on enemy supplies at Pinlebu using 4,000-lb cookies. The squadron then converted from Wellingtons to Liberators, the Wellingtons being stored prior to being scrapped between January and May 1945. Believed to be the high time, Wellington was a Mk X that managed some ninety operations, and 99 Squadron was the first FEAF bomber squadron to achieve 1,000 combat sorties.

Sharing combat duties against the Japanese with 99 Squadron was 215 Squadron. No. 215 Squadron was originally equipped with Wellington Mk Is in July 1939 at Honington, moving to Bassingbourn on 24 September 1939 where it was merged into 11 OTU on 8 April 1940 in the training role. The squadron was reformed at Newmarket on 9 December 1941, moving to Stradishall on 5 January 1942, with the ground echelon departing for India on 12 February. The squadron equipped with Wellington Mk ICs in February and departed for India on 19 March arriving on 14 April at Asanol and then Pandeveswar three days later. Detachments were made to Dum Dum and Alipore near Calcutta to be closer to targets in Burma. Accommodation was basic with one runway and no buildings, the domestic camp being under canvas. The HQ was set up in disused and derelict coal mine offices, the hot climate being uncomfortable, especially with a shortage of water for drinking and washing.

The first operational sortie for 215 Squadron was on 24 April 1942, the major deterrent to bombing being bad weather. During May, the squadron began to bomb ex-RAF airfields at Akyab and Magwe in Burma, which had become major bases for Japanese aircraft. The first raid to Magwe was a failure due to bad weather and unserviceabilities, but three Wellingtons bombed Akyab during the night of 5–6 May followed by more raids on 11 and 13 May, with modest results of three enemy aircraft damaged on the ground. Food and medical supplies were dropped to retreating Allied troops and civilians also during May.

Most raids consisted of a flight of three Wellingtons, the target on 2 June being enemy positions on Oyster Island where 12,500-lb bombs were dropped, and six aircraft were used against Japanese troop concentrations at Homalin on 6 June 1942. With the start of the monsoon in mid-June 1942, flying was even more restricted and aircraft were stuck in the mud and runway partially flooded. On 18 August, 215 Squadron moved to St Thomas Mount near Madras, starting maritime patrols off the east coast of India, which were not very productive, with no combat experiences. While retaining a detachment at St Thomas Mount, the squadron moved to Chakala on 13 October 1942. Here paratroop dropping flights were made during November with up to eight personnel being released.

The final squadron move while flying Wellingtons was to Jessore on 12 March 1943, ready for bombing operations, with increased numbers of aircraft against targets on Akyab airfield and surrounding villages. May was a bad month for the squadron with three aircraft and crews lost. In September 1943, the worn-out Mk ICs were replaced by Mk Xs with operations continuing using flare-carrying pathfinder aircraft to illuminate targets, giving improved results. In addition to bombing enemy airfields and supply dumps, during the critical siege of Imphal, 215 joined 99 Squadron in ferrying 250-lb bombs for Hurricanes to drop on the Tiddim to Imphal supply route. The squadron continued to drop supplies to Allied troops in Burma, and also loaned aircrew to support the busy Dakota units. With Wellingtons becoming outdated, conversion began to Liberators. The last Wellington operation was in early August 1944.

As in other theatres, there was a need for maritime operations in India with its vast coastline and the threat of enemy warships. The first maritime unit to operate Wellingtons was 36 Squadron, which reformed on 22 October 1942 at Tanjore with Mk ICs, although Mk VIIIs began to replace the early aircraft from February 1943. On arrival at Tanjore, the squadron personnel of five officers and 406 airmen found conditions very basic. Although there was sufficient accommodation for all personnel, there were no medical supplies, stationery, or equipment, and

Wellington named *Trichinopoly* and crews in India. (*BAE Systems*)

Wellington B IC HD954 wreck. (*BAE Systems*)

all personnel were inoculated against cholera due to a local epidemic. For local defence, they were armed with rifles, Sten guns, and ammunition. The squadron had no funds with which to pay local labour or obtain supplies. The aircraft and crews were ferried from Portreath out over the Atlantic to avoid enemy interception, approaching Gibraltar from the west. From there the route went down the West African coast to Dakar, Takoradi, and Lagos, before flying across Africa ending up in Cairo. The crews were then sent to India to reform 36 Squadron with patrols along the Burma coast. From early February, four aircraft were detached to Cholavarum, north of Madras.

On 8 April 1943, the squadron moved to Dhubalia near Calcutta, and following a quiet period in India, a move was made to Blida in the Mediterranean on 24 June where a mix of Mk Xs, XIs, XIIs, and XIIIs replaced the Mk ICs, allowing over forty sorties a month to be flown. In the place of 36 Squadron, Baltimore-equipped 203 Squadron was moved from the Mediterranean to India with sixteen Wellington Mk XIIIs arriving in Santa Cruz on 15 November 1943. The first operation was flown on 1 December providing anti-submarine protection for heavy cruiser *HMS Suffolk* during gun-firing exercises. The duties settled into the routine maritime tasks covering the shipping lanes between Bombay and Colombo, Ceylon. There were no sightings of enemy activity during the first month, but aircraft serviceability was poor due to a shortage of spares. Early in 1944, the squadron was spread widely on a number of detachments covering both Indian coasts and around Ceylon. The squadron did provide defensive coverage in April of a convoy of eleven merchant supply ships, many carrying troops with an escort of five Royal Navy ships from Aden to Bombay. A rare enemy submarine was detected on 12 July 1944 after sinking an Allied merchant ship, which was straddled with depth charges, with no further trace seen. The squadron was also used for the occasional air-sea rescue duties, but in October 1944, 203 Squadron re-equipped with Liberators at Madura.

An even more distant area of Wellington operations was the requirement to protect supply convoys around Cape Horn against U-boats in the event of Suez Canal being blocked. Along the west coast of Africa was a major route for cargo and troopships from South Africa, while the Empire Air Training Scheme in Rhodesia provided basic training for RAF aircrew away from enemy threats and poor weather in Europe. The Indian Ocean, Suez Canal, and Persian Gulf were protected by East African-based units, the choice of maritime Wellingtons being obvious. The majority of Wellingtons serving on these duties were GR Mk XIIIs although 26 (SAAF) Squadron operated five different versions.

No. 26 Squadron SAAF was formed at the trans-Africa staging point of Takoradi on the Gold Coast in May 1943. It made the first combat patrols on 29 May and the first possible U-boat contact was recorded on 15 July. The squadron was tasked with lengthy convoy escort duties that continued for many months without incident. A variation to their regular duties was the defensive cover of a battleship refuelling in the estuary of the Congo River escorted by five destroyers. The initial sortie took close to nine hours, and the cover continued for another

Maritime Wellington NZ118 with SAAF. (*RAF Museum*)

four days until the convoy sailed. Although there was no direct contact with the enemy, the Wellington patrols were effective in deterring attacks.

From 7 November, the bomb bays were reconfigured with Lindholme air-sea rescue equipment in the port side and up to nine depth charges on the starboard side. The squadron never made a successful attack on a U-boat, although Mk XI HZ526 was thought to have been shot down by gunfire from a U-boat on 18 December 1943 with the loss of the crew. On 31 March 1944, the commanding officer, Lt-Col. Nash, took a detachment of eleven Wellingtons to Ouakam near Dakar, where they joined 95 and 204 Squadron's Sunderlands in addition to Wellingtons from 344 (French) Squadron, providing continuous four-aircraft patrols between Dakar and the Cape Verde Islands. Although a U-boat was known to be in the area, it was not detected. By the end of a year of operations in May 1944, 1,232 sorties had been flown with the loss of ten aircraft and twenty-eight crew members. After a further ten months of similar operations, all routine patrols ceased on 4 March 1945; the squadron left for South Africa on 30 May and disbanded on 12 June 1945.

Allied Free French air force started Wellington coastal surveillance operations in the Groupe de Reconnaissance Maritime 'Artois' from Point Noire on 27 February 1943 with Ansons joining the force in May 1943. Following Operation Torch landings in North Africa, British and American aircraft were supplied to the French air and naval units in Algeria and Morocco. One of these was Flottille 1E, which was renumbered 344 Squadron on 29 November 1943 as part of the Free French air force under the control of 295 Wing RAF at Dakar. From July 1943, 344 Squadron was equipped with Wellington Mk XI and XIIIs for maritime patrols from Dakar-Ouakam airfield. Wellingtons were ferried from Britain to Dakar, the first to arrive being MP711, but little is known of their operations. Out of a least fifteen aircraft supplied, eight were lost, and on 18 August 1943, the only submarine to be destroyed by the squadron was *U-403* by the crew of Mk XIII HZ697, which was confirmed in January 1944. The surviving aircraft were handed over to the French on 21 June 1945, the squadron becoming Flottille 2FB on 27 November 1945.

The other regions where Wellingtons were used for maritime and general reconnaissance were East Africa and Arabia. No. 621 Squadron was formed on 18 September 1943 at Port Reitz near Mombasa in Kenya commanded by Wg Cdr P. Green. The squadron was responsible for reconnaissance over the Indian Ocean within the control of 246 Wing. The first of sixteen Wellington Mk XIIIs, HZ802, was delivered on the day the squadron was established, and moved the next day to Mogadishu ready for the first operation on 24 September. After flying for nearly ten hours on a fruitless search for a reported U-boat, a bearing was requested for return to base, but after twelve hours, the fuel was exhausted and the aircraft crash landed with one minor injury. After three days of searching, the wreck was located and the CO landed alongside to pick up the stranded crew.

The entire squadron moved to Mogadishu on 1 November 1943 to be closer to its patrol areas, and on 5 December, another move was made, this time to Khormaksar in Aden. The squadron aircraft made a number of detachments around the Arabian coastline, operating anti-submarine patrols, convoy escort, and air-sea rescue duties. It was joined by 8 Squadron in December 1943 with Wellington Mk IIIs, which also operated some Hudsons until January 1944. The maritime force was increased in February 1944 with the arrival of 244 Squadron at Sharjah in the Trucial States with Wellington Mk IIIs replacing Blenheims. No. 244 Squadron ground crews had difficulty maintaining the Wellingtons due to corrosion and minor unserviceability. The squadron moved to Masirah on 17 March 1944 with detachments at Khormaksar and Mogadishu. Despite maintaining continual convoy escort and anti-submarine patrols over a period of seventeen months, no enemy shipping was located.

Several survivors in life boats and life rafts from a sunken ship were located on 1 March by 621 Squadron, and on 1 May, the squadron recorded its only success against a U-boat. *U-852* was located by Fg Off. H. R. Mitchell in JA107 and attempted to destroy it after it had been immobilised by an 8 Squadron crew in JA413. The next day, three further Wellingtons from the squadron continued to attack the U-boat, and by 3 May, *U-852* was on fire, surrounded by wreckage and burning oil. Regular operations for both 8 and 244 Squadrons ceased in May 1945 with both disbanding on 1 May. No. 621 Squadron was transferred to a transport unit with Warwicks moving to Mersa Matruh in Egypt on 15 November 1945, with the last Wellington departing in December.

8
Multi-role Wellingtons

In addition to its outstanding role as a bomber and maritime reconnaissance aircraft, Wellingtons were also adapted for a number of other roles, both operational and non-operational. The most prominent role was for aircrew, gunnery and navigation training, which was not hazard free. Operational training has already been covered in Chapter 4, but navigation training resulted in an extended Wellington retirement until 1953. The more active operations included reconnaissance duties and special operations within 100 Group Bomber Command. No less hazardous was a range of experimental flying, while more mundane tasks were as transports.

Wellingtons had been used for general reconnaissance, but in January 1942, a six-Wellington 109 Squadron detachment at Kabrit was renumbered 162 Squadron, initially referred to as the 'Signals Squadron'. Radar reconnaissance was the main role to locate enemy radar installations and jam them, in addition to continuing jamming enemy armoured communications. Operations started on 8 January with Mk IC X9986, which flew from LG09 Bir Koraiyim to Crete where there was a signals investigation operation. The Greek islands were the initial area of interest with night time sorties used in an attempt to locate enemy radio direction finding (RDF) beacons. The first loss was Z8905 on 6 March, which failed to return from a signals investigation in the area of the Dodecanese Islands, but the crew survived to be taken prisoner. By August, the Wellington strength had reduced to just three aircraft, although two more were delivered by the end of the month. The squadron moved widely around the Mediterranean region and while based at Malta made a radar survey of Sardinia, Taranto, and Tripoli. As Allied progress in the region improved, demand for signals intelligence reduced and the squadron was deployed on occasional bombing raids, until it was disbanded on 25 September 1944.

At Benson, 544 Squadron was formed on 19 October 1942 with two Wellington Mk IVs and an assortment of other aircraft to undertake experiments in night photography. The first operation was on 15 December over northern France where photo flashes were dropped from 8,000 and 10,000 feet. The first success was achieved on 15 January 1943; the crew of Z1417 managed a series of overlapping night photos of Saint-Valery-en-Caux harbour, which were compared with similar photos taken in daylight. With their task completed the Wellingtons were withdrawn in March and replace with Mosquitos.

On 5 May 1944, 69 Squadron was moved from Malta to RAF Northolt, becoming part of the growing 2nd Tactical Air Force (TAF) in 34 Wing to cover night reconnaissance of enemy troop movements as part of the preparations for D-Day. A rigorous programme of training was required to convert the crews from their previous duties from day work with Coastal Command, to night operations over land in the RAF. Ansons were used to train navigators in night map reading and the operation of the new GEE navigation aid was introduced. The operational task was map-reading, visual reconnaissance, photography, and flare-dropping.

By May 1944, the squadron was equipped with nineteen Mk XIIIs, and the first operation was on 5 June when two aircraft were sent on a reconnaissance around the Beauvais area in France. Following the Allied D-Day landings on 6 June 1944, the major part of the operations targeted surface communications on roads and rivers and the illumination of targets by flares. The first combat loss was on the night of 10–11 June when ME902 was flying above the Le Mans to Laval road, with the loss of the crew.

Northolt-based Wellington PR XIII of 69 Squadron in 1944 used for night reconnaissance in preparation for D-Day. (*RAF Museum*)

By September, the ground situation behind the advancing Allies had improved sufficiently for operational bases to be moved to Europe, with the squadron arriving at Melsbroek near Brussels on 26 September. From here, operations continued to identify enemy road convoys with some success, with aircraft coming down from 3,000 feet to as low as 1,000 feet to achieve pictures. Despite being vulnerable during low-level night operations, particularly to enemy fighters and flak, the squadron air gunners fired on a Bf 109 on 19 December and an unidentified aircraft damaged a Me 410 shot down on Christmas Day. When flying on clear moonlit nights, 250-lb bombs were carried to be more on the offensive. Most sorties were around one hour twenty minutes with each crew flying up to three sorties a night, providing good intelligence for the Allied armies of enemy troop and armoured locations.

However, the squadron lost a number of aircraft on the ground during German offensive Operation Bodenplatte on New Year's Day 1945, which was a last-ditch attack on Allied airfields in Holland and Belgium. Eleven Wellingtons were among the many aircraft destroyed and two badly damaged. Although no aircrew were killed, five ground crew were killed and twenty-five others injured. Recovery was rapid with new aircraft ferried from Britain and Wellington bombing operations starting once again from the night of 4–5 January. By March 1945, all reconnaissance was visual, and with a reduction in potential targets in April, operations wound down. During that month, the squadron worked with the Royal Navy in location and destruction of enemy one-man submarines with four aircraft detached at Knocke on the Belgian coast, but without success. Operations ceased on 7 May, the squadron moving to Aalborg in Denmark in July for survey work before disbanding at Eindhoven in Holland on 7 August 1945.

Transport operations with converted Wellington bomber versions may have appeared more mundane, but still created hazards due to weather and operational challenges. Some fifty-nine conversions are known to have been made during bomber production including C Mk Is, C Mk IXs, C Mk XVs, and C Mk XVIs, while over 100 were converted in the field and at maintenance units. A number of these conversions were attached to station and communication flights as well as used as VIP transports for senior officers and staff. All bomb bay equipment was removed with bomb doors sealed and a lined cabin fitted along the interior of the fuselage, with windows along the sides. Up to nine passengers could be carried or eighteen troops. The initial conversion was Mk IC P2522 emerging as a C Mk IX for the Airborne Forces Experimental Establishment (AFEE) at Sherburn in Elmet. Mk I L4255 was converted to an air ambulance for the Air Transport Auxiliary (ATA) at White Waltham.

BOAC operated the Air Despatch Letter Service (ADLS) to Malta, and in August 1940, this was taken over by Hendon-based 24 Squadron using three converted Wellington Mk ICs among other transport types. For this operation, the bomb racks and associated wiring were removed, and a long cylindrical fuel tank installed to cover the longer range to Malta. Other destinations included Northern Ireland from July 1940, and Gibraltar from April 1942. Wellingtons

Multi-role Wellingtons 181

Pegasus-powered unarmed passenger Wellington C XVI N2875 converted from B IC in August 1944. (*BAE Systems*)

Wellington C XVI R2990 *Duke of Montrose* ZK-D from 24 Squadron Hendon, 1942–1943. (*BAE Systems*)

Wellington C XVI NQ-A *Duke of Rutland* from 24 Squadron, 1943–1945. (*BAE Systems*)

were also introduced to 232 and 242 Squadrons in Transport Command, but they were withdrawn in February when they were replaced by the more suitable Liberators and Stirlings.

In more remote parts of the world, the only practical method of transport was by air, but with priority given to combat types, there was a shortage of transport aircraft. An example was RAF Middle East in 1941 where a number of Wellington Mk Is, Mk IIs, Mk IIIs, and Mk IVs were converted to the transport role by removing all the bombing equipment, armaments, and fitting seats. This task was later taken over by Vickers with more than 100 reconfigured. Although unarmed, some were painted with mock turrets and fitted with dummy guns. In a VIP layout, there was a cabin with twelve seats aft, and forward, there were three seats for fitter, rigger, and the AVM's driver. The Communications Squadron of the 3rd Tactical Air Force in Burma were equipped with Mk Xs and Mk XIIIs at Comilla during 1943 and 1944, used mainly for dropping supplies over the front lines.

There was a need for passenger-carrying aircraft in occupied Italian Eritrea, and from September 1942, four Wellington Mk ICs were loaned to BOAC by the RAF. These aircraft were originally intended for the SAAF, and although BOAC had been formed on 1 November 1939, the aircraft carried British Airways titles. Conversion to the new configuration involved removing all armament with the front and rear turrets faired over. The bomb release system, oxygen system, and auxiliary oil tanks were also removed. Bench seats were installed for sixteen passengers who entered via steps through a hatch in the forward fuselage by the pilot's seat. Baggage and freight were located in the nose turret compartment with a loading hatch in the extreme nose and separated from the pilot by a removable bulkhead. As no emergency exits were available, the aircraft could not be awarded a civil certificate of airworthiness (C of A) and therefore retained their military identities. The aircraft were also flown by RAF aircrew, and were based at Almaza in Cairo as part of the BOAC No. 5 Line, with scheduled services beginning on 26 October 1942.

Weekly services were from Cairo to Karachi via Lydda, Habbaniyah, Shaibah, Bahrain, Sharjah, and Jiwani, which operated until May 1943, and there was also a weekly Cairo to Basra service via Lydda, which was flown until 8 November 1942. Following the Battle of El Alamein, Wellingtons were also used on *ad hoc* operations into the desert including Mersa Matruh, El Adem, and Marble Arch. There was a plan to increase the fleet to twelve Wellingtons, but this was not carried through due to the poor performance of the initial four combat-weary ex-RAF aircraft. There had been difficulty maintaining the aircraft due to lack of spares and rudimentary engineering facilities. The four Wellingtons remained with BOAC until July 1943, when they were replaced by more practical Dakotas, and were passed on to 28 Squadron SAAF.

On 1 June 1943, 28 Squadron SAAF was formed at Castel Benito with the four ex-BOAC Mk ICs and some Ansons, with the Wellingtons being a stop gap until Dakotas became available. The first three Wellingtons were delivered on 19 July, with the fourth arriving on 28 July. The aircraft were in poor condition and continued to be difficult to maintain, with engine failures being common, making the value of the aircraft doubtful. By 13 August, only two remained airworthy, and much of the unserviceability was due to a lack of spares. The remaining two aircraft were finally withdrawn in December and both scrapped soon after.

The Balkan Air Force Communications Flight based at Bari was equipped with Mk Xs from October 1944 to July 1945. These aircraft were used for transporting people and medical supplies.

Between December 1942 and September 1945, the Fleet Air Arm (FAA) of the Royal Navy were allocated twenty-four Wellingtons of different marks for duties with second line naval air squadrons (NAS). The major operator was Lee-on-Solent-based 765 NAS, which dispersed the Wellingtons to the longer runway at Manston where crew training started in August 1944 and the last of eight were withdrawn in April 1946. The major role of the squadron was as a mobile recording unit assessing the efficiency of radar systems. The aircraft were also used occasionally for long range reconnaissance. In October 1945, the squadron was posted to Malta to assist in picking up Allied troops from around the Mediterranean prior to being sent home to Britain by sea. No. 758 NAS, the Naval Advanced Instrument Flying School based at Hinstock, used Wellingtons; 762 NAS at Dale used the aircraft for twin-engine conversion; and 783 NAS based at Arbroath was tasked with ASV training. Other FAA units were 716 NAS with Mk XIs from July 1944 to September 1945 when it was disbanded, 778 NAS at Crail with Mk IIs, and 782 NAS at Donibristle in December 1942 with Mk I and Mk IIs.

On 4 January 1943, 192 Squadron was formed at Gransden Lodge by renumbering 1474 Flight. The initial equipment of the squadron consisted of Wellington Mks IC, II, and X in addition to Mosquito Mk IVs. The secret duties of the squadron included providing enemy radar countermeasures by identifying patterns and wavelengths. Research flights were operated over Germany and occupied Europe in support of Bomber Command raids. The squadron also operated over the Bay of Biscay and the Mediterranean. On 5 April 1943, the squadron moved to Feltwell, and on 25 November, a further move was made to Foulsham when it became part of 100 Bomber Support Group, operating with Wellingtons even when the type had been withdrawn from the main bomber offensive.

An operational example was on the night of 30–31 March 1944, when Bomber Command lost more aircraft mainly to enemy night fighters than any other time during the war. Out of 795 bombers despatched, ninety-six were lost, a total which was unsustainable. During this raid, one 192 Squadron Wellington took off from Ford to investigate the Knickebein enemy radio beam navigation aid, which was picked up 25 miles from the English coast, and created countermeasures, rendering the beam ineffective. The squadron disbanded on 22 August 1945 to become the Central Signals Establishment and Radio Warfare Establishment.

A rather more mundane task for Wellingtons was glider-towing. Initial trials were conducted by the Airborne Forces Establishment at Sherburn in Elmet in 1942 with Mk IC DV942, which was used as a tug for General Aircraft Hotspur training gliders. Trials continued later in the year with more powerful Mk III X3286 and Mk X HE731, which could tow the larger Horsa and Hadrian troop-carrying gliders. However, there was concern that the lack of rigidity of the Wellington geodetic structure could result in stretching under such heavy loads, with further development in this role being abandoned.

Wellingtons were found to be ideal platforms for trials and development of a number of experimental weapons and systems. Perhaps the most famous were the trials of Highball bouncing bomb for use against enemy capital ships by 618 Squadron RAF. Highball was a smaller version of the Upkeep used on the Dams raid by 617 Squadron, and under development at the same time. A planned target was the German battleship *Tirpitz* sheltering in a Norwegian fiord—a major threat to Allied shipping. As an initial test of this weapon, Wellington Mk III BJ895 was flown over Chesil Beach on 4 December 1942 by Vickers chief test pilot Mutt Summers with inventor Barnes Wallis as bomb aimer. The bomb doors had been removed and inert weapons were used, but following release, they broke up on impact with the sea. When filled with explosive, although referred to as a bomb, it was in fact a depth charge, which was rotated and when impacted with a target ship it sank down the hull and was exploded by a hydrostatic fuse. The spinning kept the weapon close to the ship's hull and when it exploded, the surrounding water cushioned the explosion, forcing the main charge forward into the target.

Broughton-built Wellington BJ895 was delivered to Vickers on 12 August 1943, with the trials rounds dropped being inert only, with drops at both Chesil

Beach and Reculver in the Thames Estuary. The aircraft also visited Turnberry in Scotland during April 1943 for familiarisation by the Skitten-based 618 Squadron crews, where a pair of Highballs would be carried in tandem in a modified Mosquito B IV bomb bay. On completion of Highball trials, BJ895 was returned to standard configuration and was delivered to the Marine Aircraft Experimental Establishment (MAEE). It later was issued to the Central Gunnery School (CGS), but was written off on 24 July 1946 when it crashed at Wykeham Abbey in Yorkshire, during a fighter affiliation exercise.

The Wellington proved a useful aircraft for the early testing of Britain's pioneer jet engines being developed by Frank Whittle's Power Jets. Wellington Mk II Z8570 was withdrawn from RAF service in May 1942 and modified by Vickers to carry a W2B jet engine installation in the extreme tail. Following structural modifications, the aircraft was flown to the Rolls-Royce test airfield at Hucknall where the test engine was fitted by early August 1942, and cleared for flight on 12 August. A crew of four were carried and flight trials started with two flights on 14 August, the engine running satisfactorily during the second flight. One of the four crew members was an observer located in the rear fuselage monitoring the jet engine performance.

On 1 February 1943, the aircraft was taken to altitude for the first time reaching 23,500 feet. With the added weight of the engine in the extreme rear, the centre of gravity was extreme aft, causing handling difficulties for the pilot, especially in the landing configuration with full flaps. Captain Ronald 'Shep' Sheperd, the Rolls-Royce chief test pilot, had to use all his strength to maintain control. The extra rearward weight also caused regular failures of the tailwheel fork structure. A further nine W2Bs were tested between September 1943 and November 1944 with 302 flights and a total time of 456 hours. The aircraft was struck off charge in October 1945.

With the increasing need for jet engine development, Wellington W5797 was also modified and allocated to Rolls-Royce at Hucknall, flying 195 hours with nine engine changes, after which it was used for ground trials from 19 September 1942. It was replaced in flight trials by W5389 with its first W2B fitted at the end of June 1943, with the ultimate high-altitude test being to 35,000 feet on 13 March 1944, when the engine performed well. During a subsequent high-altitude test on 28 December 1944, the oxygen system failed at 30,000 feet. The Rolls-Royce chief test pilot, Sqn Ldr Jim Heywood, began to feel the effects of oxygen starvation an hour into the flight, but managed to warn his flight test observer before beginning to lose consciousness. The observer also began to black out, but luckily, he was able to find an emergency oxygen bottle, which he gave to the unconscious pilot before passing out. When they both began to regain consciousness, the aircraft was at 28,000 feet in a shallow dive, at 250 mph. Control was regained at 20,000 feet and a safe landing made at Hucknall.

With the additional power from the jet engine, the Wellington had a significant increase in speed and performance at altitude was very effective. One rumoured example was when the Wellington was in the descent, a Spitfire was seen at

Wellington II W5389/G fitted with Whittle W.2B jet engine in tail. (*BAE Systems*)

Whittle W.2/700 jet engine installation in Wellington II W5518/G tail. (*BAE Systems*)

Whittle W.2B jet engine installation in Wellington B II Z8570/G. (*Newark Air Museum*)

29,000 feet. The jet engine was restarted, and the Spitfire pilot was surprised to be overtaken by a Wellington with both propellers feathered. With higher performance aircraft required for jet engine advancing research, W5389 was retired in June 1947.

Power Jets (Research and Development) established a flight development unit at Bruntingthorpe in Leicester near to their Rugby HQ on 11 September 1944. Following the initial test, Lancaster Mk II—a hybrid Merlin-powered Wellington Mk II/VI—W5518 was fitted with a Whittle W2/700 turbojet. As before, this ex-RAF aircraft was modified by Vickers, including 465-gallon paraffin fuel tanks in the bomb bay, making its first flight from Weybridge on 24 November 1944 and delivered to Bruntingthorpe on 17 December. In May 1946, the testing became the responsibility of the National Gas Turbine Establishment (NGTE), and on 14 May, the aircraft moved to its new home at Bitteswell and was finally scrapped on 30 November 1948.

Wellington Mk 10 LN715 was acquired by Rolls-Royce in 1948 for use as a flying test bed for the Dart turboprop, to be used to power the Vickers Viscount and other aircraft types. The significant modification programme, including provision for jet fuel, was made by Vickers at Weybridge before delivery to Hucknall on 13 October 1948. At the end of the test programme with no further use required, the aircraft was withdrawn in April 1952. Similarly, Mk 10 LN718 was used by Bristol at Filton as a flying test bed for the Hercules engine driving a four-blade propeller to power the Vickers Viking. Napier at Luton used Wellington Mk 10 NA857 as a flying test bed for the Naiad turboprop, and although Naiad

Wellington Mk 10 LN715 powered by a pair of Rolls-Royce Dart turboprop engines. (*RAF Museum*)

Rolls-Royce Dart turboprop engine in Wellington Mk 10 LN715. (*BAE Systems*)

Rolls-Royce Dart turboprop installation in Wellington Mk 10 LN715. (*BAE Systems*)

engines were fitted, the aircraft was replaced by a more suitable Avro Lincoln. The Wellington never flew with the development engines and it was disposed of in November 1949.

During the Second World War, Vickers carried out a great deal of experimental test flying, much of it related to progressive development of new versions and related equipment. However, among the more advanced ideas was the plan to fit an offensive 40-mm 'S' gun as mid upper armament. The idea was first suggested in 1938 and approved for go ahead the next year with Mk II L4250 selected for the trials. The centre fuselage was strengthened to carry the large turntable and structure to support the weapon and the hydraulic motors to power it. The first flight with the installation was made in 1940, but there was severe vibration and control difficulties caused by the disturbed airflow, resulting in the standard fin and rudder being replaced by a dual unit. The aircraft was sent to the Air Gun Mounting Establishment (AGME) at Duxford on 13 December 1941 for service trials. It moved to A&AEE at Boscombe Down on 24 January 1942 where it was fired for the first time over Lyme Bay on 8 March. During subsequent firings, it was found that at low elevations, fabric was torn off the wing. The requirement was not followed up, and in late 1942, the aircraft was fitted with a defensive mid-upper turret armed with four 0.5-inch guns. At the conclusion of these tests, the aircraft was scrapped by the end of the year.

A nose-mounted 40-mm gun was tested in Mk II Z8416, which started flight trials on 3 November 1944, but following initial handling tests, the project was cancelled and the aircraft struck off charge in 1946.

Wellington Mk II prototype L4250 with 40-mm cannon installation in upper rear fuselage, fitted with the standard single fin and rudder June 1941. (*RAF Museum*)

Wellington Mk II L4250 with experimental 40-mm cannon installation on rear fuselage and fitted with twin fins and rudders to improve stability in January 1942. (*RAF Museum*)

Wellington Mk II L4250 with 40-mm cannon trial installation in October 1941. (*RAF Museum*)

Although the Fighter Interception Unit (FIU) based at Ford was originally established to test new night fighter radars, its role was later expanded to include other roles resulting in Wellingtons being included in the fleet. One Wellington was used as a target to evaluate the Lichtenstein AI radar installed in a captured Luftwaffe Ju 88R-1 night fighter. The Farnborough-based Wellington carried out a variety of evasion manoeuvres in daylight, but the Wellington was not representative of RAF heavy four-engined bombers due to its greater evasive actions. Wellington T XVIII ND129 was fitted with AI radar in place of the front nose gun turret and served with the FIU in the spring of 1945.

Also used for radar development was Wellington Mk XIII NB823, which was delivered to FIU on 12 June 1944, but this was H2D surface-mapping radar with initial trials being made at Defford using NB822. H2D was a development of H2S, designed to detect movements of road traffic at night. The trials were flown in daylight along stretches of fairly straight roads at an altitude of 3,000 feet. Over sixteen flights, an observer in the nose kept a log of observations visually to compare with those detected by the H2D operation's report. The maximum range for the detection of vehicles was found to be 3 miles, and it was found the aircraft must not wander more than 300 yards from either side of the road or traffic would not be detected. The system's accuracy was found to be around 60

Hercules XVII-powered Wellington T XVIII ND129 ZQ-R FIU on 10 April 1945, used for training night fighter crews. (*RAF Museum*)

per cent when compared with actual observations, and false signals were given by trees and other obstacles along the road side. With overall accuracy no better than 50 per cent, it was decided that accuracy would have to much improved to make H2D operational. Wellington Mk 10 RP468 was used briefly by Airwork for radar trials to the Norwegian coastline. It was registered G-ALUH with a C of A issued on 22 July 1949 and the radar was fitted in the tail in place of the rear gun turret. The registration was cancelled on 11 October and the aircraft returned to the RAF.

Wellington Mk X RP468 radar antenna in tail. (*BAE Systems*)

Wellington Mk X RP468 with radar antenna in the tail. (*BAE Systems*)

Wellington T 10 G-ALUH with radar in the tail for trials with Airwork. (*BAE Systems*)

9

Post-War Service

At the end of the Second World War in May 1945, the RAF had a surplus amounting to a total of over 9,000 aircraft, resulting in entire fleets being withdrawn as no longer required, examples being Hawker Typhoons and American Lend-Lease types such as Lockheed Neptunes, which by the end of 1945 were no longer in service. There were also well over 1 million personnel, of which 193,000 were aircrew, many of whom were released from service. While a number of aircrew signed up for permanent commissions, there was a need for aircrew to be recruited to replace the older members in the service, and some aircraft such as the Wellington were retained.

The last Wellington to be built was Mk 10 RP590 from the Blackpool production line was delivered on 13 October 1945 and issued to 1 (Pilot) Refresher Flying Training Unit at Finningley. This unit became the Flying Refresher School on 1 June 1949, the task being to provide regular pilots with updated flying experience to prepare them for new aircraft developments and operating procedures. Among the aircraft used were eleven Wellington Mk 10s. It was redesignated No. 101 Flying Refresher School on 1 April 1951, still flying Wellington Mk 10s helping with the RAF expansion for the Korean War, disbanding 1 February 1952 by which time Wellingtons had been withdrawn.

With the end of the war, large numbers of bomber crews were no longer required and released from service with the disbandment of the majority of the OTUs by the end of 1945, the last withdrawn by autumn of 1946. The slimmed down post-war RAF training system needed to be optimised for the ever-changing air force, particularly with the introduction of jet-powered aircraft. The OTUs were therefore replaced by advanced flying schools (AFS), followed by conversion units for each major service type. Wellingtons continued with AFS units with Mk 10s equipping 201 AFS, which formed at Swinderby, and 202 AFS, which formed at Finningley, both on 15 March 1947. The role of the two AFSs was to

Last Wellington Mk 10, RP468, outside the Blackpool factory ready for delivery on 13 October 1945. (*RAF Museum*)

Hercules-powered Wellington T 10 RP589 with rear gun turret in January 1949. (*RAF Museum*)

Wellington T 10 RP589 front three-quarters in January 1949. (*BAE Systems*)

provide training for crews of multi-engined aircraft. The major equipment was Wellington Mk 10s, the two AFSs combining at Swinderby on 1 December 1947. The Wellingtons were replaced by Varsities from October 1951.

With large numbers of surplus low hour aircraft available, some 270 earlier versions were converted to T Mk 10 standards by Boulton Paul Aircraft at Wolverhampton between January 1946 and March 1952. Theses conversions retained the bomb bay and rear turret to cover bomb aimer and gunnery instruction. At various times between May 1945 and February 1952, five Wellington-equipped air navigation schools (ANS) were established. No. 1 ANS was 9 April 1947 at Topcliffe with twenty-one Wellington Mk 10s; No. 2 ANS formed on 4 June 1947 at Bishops Court also with twenty-one Mk 10s; No. 5 ANS formed at Jurby on 31 May 1945; 7 ANS formed on 31 May 1945 at Bishops Court; and 10 ANS formed on 11 June 1945 at Dumfries.

Due to an increased requirement for navigators with the build-up of the Cold War and with the Korean War, two more were established—5 ANS reforming on 5 March 1951 at Lindholm, having previously disbanded 9 April 1947, and 6 ANS at Lichfield on 15 February 1952. The crew typically consisted of a pilot, radio operator, training navigator, and up to four trainee navigators. Training was by day and night flying at low level and up to 12,000 feet, all around the UK.

Swinderby-based Wellington T 10 PG314 FMA-L from 201 AFS. (*BAE Systems*)

Wellington T 10 NA928 in June 1949, ready for delivery to the RAF for training. (*RAF Museum*)

Bishops Court-based Wellington T 10 LFO-X from 7 ANS. (*BAE Systems*)

Jurby-based Wellington T 10 FFK-F from 5 ANS. (*BAE Systems*)

Bishops Court-based Wellington T 10 LP361 FFO-Y from 2 ANS. (*BAE Systems*)

Wellington T 10 NC425 FFO-F from 2 ANS. (*BAE Systems*)

To give a break from routine flying training, the ANS Wellingtons could be called on to participate in exercises, an example being Exercise Foil in July 1949, where Wellingtons were returned to bomber duties to test air defences. The aircraft still suffered from unreliability, particularly with the engines, and at higher altitudes, they could be cold and draughty. Blind approaches were practiced using Rebecca BABS (blind approach beacon system), which proved to be very accurate, and although GEE was available, it was not used much due to making navigation too easy. Training had to allow for the most difficult and basic conditions. The crews practiced bomb aiming and photography during day and night. As an extra challenge, the basic autopilot known as 'George' was unreliable, as well as the central compass system, the training being very much based on outdated Second World War equipment.

More specialised Wellington Mks 17 and 18 were used for training Mosquito night fighter navigators with a SCR720 AI radar located in place of the front gun turret. The eighty T Mk XVIIIs were new build aircraft, while nine T Mk XVIIs were conversions of T Mk Xs. These aircraft were used in the latter stages of the Second World War with 51 OTU from March 1944 at Cranfield, 54 OTU from February 1945 at Charterhall, and 62 OTU with twenty-nine Mks XVII/XVIII at Ouston from March 1945. Two T Mk 18s served with the Central Fighter Establishment (CFE) at West Raynham and the last seven of this mark were with 228 OCU at Leeming until replaced by Valettas from October 1956.

The last Wellington version was the T Mk 19, which was a conversion from the Mk 10 in 1946 for the role of basic aircrew trainer. During 1948, twenty-four Mk 10s were to be converted at 24 MU at Stoke Heath, but only six were completed before the programme was cancelled. The completed aircraft were ferried from Tern Hill for storage at 8 MU Little Rissington in December 1948 and were later scrapped with no further service.

Crew training still continued to be a high risk with a number of fatalities caused by accidents, including mid-air collisions. On 17 March 1948, a pair of 1 ANS Wellington T 10s collided in the circuit at Topcliffe. While RP499 was joining the circuit, RP565 was taking off. Both aircraft were making left turns, and the pilots were unable to see each other, one falling on the station sergeant's mess, killing all eight crew members. Following this accident, the resulting investigation recommended that the right-hand seat should be occupied to provide a look-out. Lessons were still being learned even at this stage in Wellington operations. A second less disastrous mid-air collision was between 2 ANS Wellington Mk 10 NC925 on 20 June 1952 when there was a collision with a Meteor T7, which just descended out of cloud. All four crew of the Wellington were able to parachute to safety. The hazards of training were once again confirmed when T Mk 10 NA598 was on a navigation exercise to Gibraltar from Shawbury. It should have avoided overflying Spain, but due to bad weather, it hit Montgó Mountain near Alicante in Northern Spain on 5 December 1950, killing all seven crew.

With a need for improved navigator training in new equipment becoming available, Wellingtons were no longer able to keep pace. It was rapidly replaced

Wellington T XVII NC869 from 35 CGS in April 1945. (*BAE Systems*)

Wellington T XVII, converted from T X for Mosquito night fighter navigator training. (*BAE Systems*)

Wellington T XVIII NC928 in November 1944, ready for delivery for training of Mosquito night fighter navigators. (*RAF Museum*)

Wellington T 19 RP318, one of only six converted from T 10s and never used. (*BAE Systems*)

at the ANSs by Valettas for basic advanced navigator training and Varsities for advanced training from 1953. Wellington aerodynamics was not abandoned as the Valetta featured a similar wing with metal skin, and similar tail and undercarriage, but the fuselage was a new metal stressed skin construction. The new fuselage of both types provided much more room and were more suitably configured for student training, the Varsity having a nose wheel undercarriage and a bomb-aiming pannier under the fuselage.

The final training unit to use Wellington Mk 10s was 1 ANS at Hullavington, where on the strength was MF628, now preserved at the RAF Museum, and managed to escape the mass scrapping at 8 MU Little Rissington. During February 1953, many of the redundant Wellingtons were ferried to 8 MU, which had been responsible for support of the aircraft and by the end of 1945 had 1,388 stored, either at Little Rissington or the satellites at Honeybourne and Long Marston from 1 ANS in March 1953. MF628 survived, as it was selected from storage at St Athan to fly in making the film *The Dam Busters*. It returned to St Athan on 14 October 1954 and was flown to the Vickers airfield at Wisley on 24 January 1955, the final flight of a Wellington. It appeared in the fiftieth RAF anniversary celebrations at Abingdon and earmarked for preservation as the then sole surviving complete example of this significant bomber. Some grounded examples were being used for engineering training until the mid-1950s, but none survived to be preserved.

Out of a total production run of 11,462 Wellingtons built, 1,727 were lost in combat with over 9,000 crew members killed, wounded, or taken prisoner. Wellington crews made a total of 47,409 sorties with Bomber Command, dropping nearly 42,000 tons of bombs. In addition, 337 more Wellingtons and aircrews were lost in the hazards of training. Despite the high price paid, the surviving crews were proud of their achievements, even though they were overshadowed by the major four-engined heavy bombers which replaced Wellingtons in service with Bomber Command and on coastal duties.

Wellington T 10 NA829 from Hullavington with 1 ANS. (*Author's collection*)

Wellington T 10 NA851 with bomb doors partly open and a rear gun turret. (*BAE Systems*)

Wellington T 10 MF628, which became the only complete original Wellington to be preserved and served with 1 ANS at Hullavington. (*RAF Museum*)

10

Foreign Air Forces

In addition to overseas service with the RAF, Wellingtons were also flown by Allied air arms after the Second World War and the enemy during hostilities. The French Air Force (*L'Armee de l'Air*) had received 185 ex-RAF aircraft by 1946 to help rebuild their depleted aircraft stocks. There appears to have been little use of the aircraft by the air force, although some Mk 16s were believed to be modified as transports for service in French Indochina. However, greater use of these aircraft was made by the Aeronavale, following a number used from October 1944 for non-pilot and engineering training by the *Ecole de Premier Vol* (EPV) at Thiersville in Algeria. Some of the RAF aircraft supplied to *L'Armee de l'Air* were mostly passed on to EPV, which was redesignated 52S on 11 October 1948 based at Lartigue, Madaillan, moving to Agadir, Morocco in 1951. Some of the Wellingtons were operated in the maritime reconnaissance role based at Lanvéoc-Poulmic with Esc 1S from November 1944. In addition, Flottille 2F was formed from the Free French 344 Squadron RAF in November 1945 at Dakar-Ouakam, Senegal, moving to Port Lyautey, Morocco, in June 1950.

No. 51S was also formed in 1946 in Morocco. The duty of these units was to help clear German mines still around French coastlines, a task which continued until the end of 1951. Following the loss of Mk 11 MP696 on 8 June 1951 with the death of the commanding officer and crew of five, the withdrawal was hastened and Lancasters were supplied as replacements. Both 52S and 56S operated some twenty Wellington GR 13s and GR 14s, with the final operators being 56S in Agadir and 55S at Goéland, then Port Lyautey, with one or two still flying as late as 1955.

The Royal Hellenic Air Force was supplied with some twenty Wellingtons, including Mk 10s, and sixteen Mk 13s between November 1944 and April 1946. They were issued to 13 Squadron, based near Athens for training and transport duties in addition to some ASV crew training. Due to having been stored in the desert for some time, the aircraft were in poor condition and difficult to maintain, suffering two fatal accidents. One was Mk 13 MF188 while on an air test on 10 April 1946 when it spun into the sea with the loss of all on board. The other was Mk 13 MF466, which stalled on approach to Eleusis on 7 August 1946. Some aircraft suffered minor damage, but they were not economical to repair and were scrapped. Following renumbering to 355 Squadron, Dakotas began to replace the Wellingtons from October 1946, and the last was broken up in 1947.

The only dominion to operate Wellingtons was South Africa with 17 Squadron SAAF reformed at Gianaclis in May 1945 with plans to move to Asia. Eight Wellington Mk 10s were supplied for crew training in preparation for equipping with eleven improved Warwicks. The Wellingtons were only flown occasionally due to poor weather and low serviceability. They were withdrawn in September after only four months of service.

A number of Wellingtons made forced-landings in enemy territory, probably mostly due to engine problems. Some were evaluated by the Luftwaffe—an example being Mk IA L8899 of 301 Squadron, which force-landed in Holland on 24 September 1940 while on an operation to Berlin, the crew becoming POWs. Another example was Mk IC T2501 of 99 Squadron, which landed at Vitry-en-Artois on 5 December 1940 after being damaged by flak with the six crew becoming POWs. This aircraft carried full German markings including the code '5+4' to avoid destruction by 'friendly fire'. Mk IC L7842 of 311 (Czech) Squadron made a forced-landing during an attack on Boulogne on 7 February 1941; although it retained its squadron codes, it had German markings and was evaluated at the Luftwaffe test centre at Rechlin.

11

Preserved Wellingtons

One of the most demanding restorations of any historic aircraft was Wellington Mk IA N2980:R of 20 OTU by volunteers at the Brooklands Museum. Built at Brooklands by Vickers, 'Mutt' Summers, the chief test pilot, made the first production test flight on 16 November 1939. Following completion of its flight test schedule, the aircraft was delivered four days later to 149 Squadron at Mildenhall where it was marked OJ-R—*R for Robert*. The first combat operation was on 18 December when N2980 was one of twenty-eight Wellingtons from IX, 37, and 149 Squadrons on the Battle of Heligoland Bight, from which only ten Wellingtons returned, one being *R for Robert*. N2980 joined 37 Squadron at Feltwell on 30 May 1940, flying fourteen operations before being modified to Mk IC standard when it left 37 Squadron and was delivered to 20 OTU on 6 October at Lossiemouth.

On New Year's Eve 1940, the aircraft took off from Lossiemouth on a navigation exercise with the eight crew and Sqn Ldr David Marwood Elton in command plus Plt Off. J. F. Slatter as co-pilot. Both were regular instructors at 20 OTU with the six students with the rank of sergeant learning their respective operational skills. The student navigators were C. Chandler, E. Ford, R. E. Little, and Lucton with wireless operator/air gunner W. Wright and rear gunner J. S. Fensome. The additional challenge was appalling weather with no sign of improvement.

The captain headed south-west at the southern end of Loch Ness, climbing to 8,000 feet to give safe clearance from the surrounding mountains. They were flying in dense cloud with threatening snow squalls, when the starboard Pegasus XVIII engine failed. With the aircraft descending, Marwood-Elton ordered the rear crew to abandon the aircraft, but it took some time for them all to clear, resulting in both pilots still being in the doomed aircraft at low altitude. Suddenly, Marwood-Elton spotted a gap in the clouds with a dark stretch of black water surface below. He believed a force-landing on water was preferable to coming down by parachute into the unknown. The touchdown on the water was perfect allowing both pilots to get out and into their dinghy to paddle ashore with *R for Robert* sinking into the depths of Loch Ness.

While the trainee navigators and wireless operator bailed out successfully, the rear gunner Fensome may have pulled his ripcord too soon and, damaging his parachute on the tailplane, fell to his death. To underline the hazards of combat only two of the crew members survived the war, one being wireless operator/air gunner Wright, and the captain of N2980. Chandler died on 2 August 1941. Flt Sgt Little was navigator on Stirling N3754 of 7 Squadron; he was shot down by a night fighter on the night of 25–26 June 1942 during a 1,000 bomber raid on Bremen. Three members of the crew survived to become POWs, but the four, including Little, were killed.

By now a flight lieutenant, Slatter was captain of a 105 Squadron Mosquito IV (DZ548) of 105 Squadron at Marham on 5 February 1944, which collided with a USAAF B-17G of the 96th Bomb Group. The two Mosquito crew were killed, but the B-17 was able to return to base. On 22 March 1944, David Marwood-Elton, by now group captain DFC commanding RAF Burn, was with 578 Squadron Halifax LW540 on a raid to Frankfurt, which was shot down by a Ju 88; all the eight crew became POWs. David died in 1995 aged eighty-four, but not before he witnessed the recovery of his Wellington from Loch Ness in September 1985.

Wellington N2980 *R for Robert* was located by chance by a team using modern sonar-locating equipment in an attempt to find any trace of the mystical Loch Ness Monster. No trace of the monster was found, but an aircraft wreck, believed to be a Catalina, was located 7 m deep. Heriot Watt University in Edinburgh was in the process of developing a remotely operated vehicle (ROV) for the offshore oil industry, and it was felt the recovery of the aircraft wreck would be a useful practical exercise for the new ROV. The images recovered showed that the aircraft was not a Catalina, but a Wellington, and a Royal Navy diving team confirmed it was N2980.

After many years underwater, *R for Robert* was deteriorating and the publicity made it a target for divers with souvenir hunters threatening it. With the support of Heriot Watt University, a charity was established in 1984 to salvage the wreck. On a second attempt, the Wellington was raised to the surface on 21 September 1985. Six days later, the remains of N2980 were delivered by British Aerospace back to Brooklands where it had been built. Then started the long and painstaking task of restoring the aircraft to as near as possible to the condition it was in when it was delivered to the RAF. During restoration, new sections of geodetic structure were made, the aircraft was raised on its undercarriage, and the engines were installed with distorted propellers from its final landing on the water's surface. The flight deck, along with the navigator's and wireless operator's equipment, has been refitted, together with nose and tail gun turrets. The only non-standard part of the restoration was to leave large sections of the airframe uncovered to demonstrate the rugged geodetic structure developed by its designer, Dr Barnes Wallis, who later went on the design the bouncing bomb Upkeep used on the Dams raid.

Preserved Wellingtons

Wellington B I N2980 preserved at Brooklands showing the construction. (*Author's photo*)

Wellington B I N2980 centre-section from above preserved at Brooklands. (*Author's photo*)

Wellington B I N2980 rear view showing partly fabric covered fuselage. (*Author's photo*)

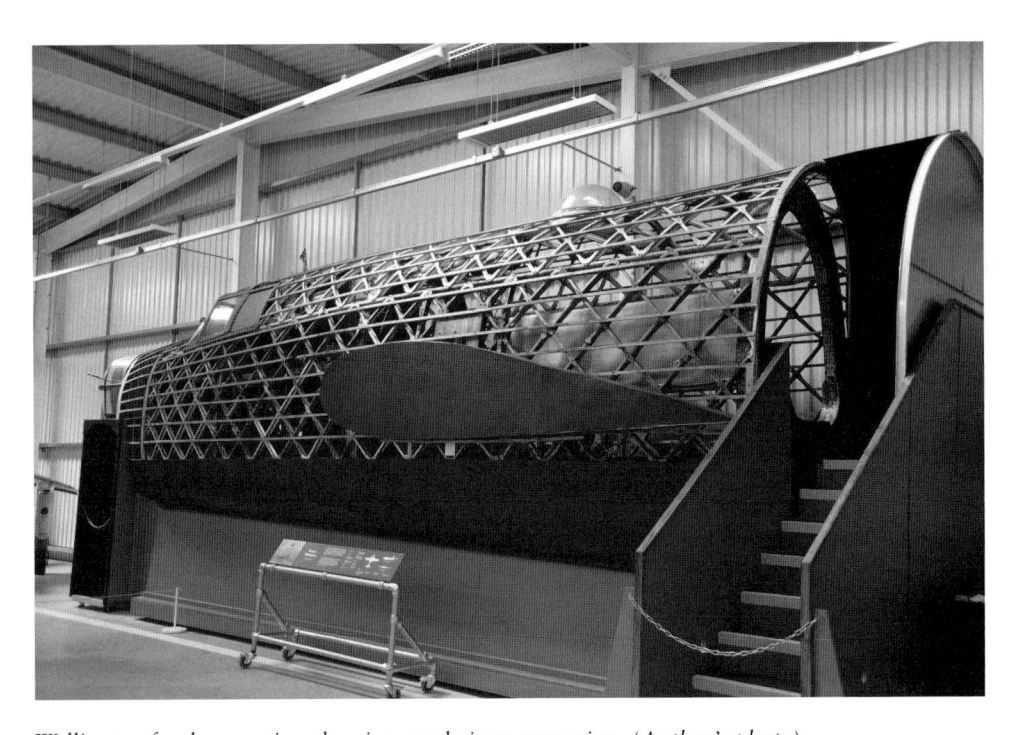

Wellington fuselage section showing geodetic construction. (*Author's photo*)

The RAF Museum's example had a more mundane existence. Built at Blackpool, MF628 first flew on 9 May 1944 and was converted to a T Mk 10 by Boulton Paul in March 1948. It was delivered to 1 ANS at Hullavington in April 1949 where it was used for navigation training until going to 19 MU at St Athan for storage on 28 October 1952. It was maintained in flying condition and made at least two air show appearances, one at the RAeS Garden Party at Hatfield in June 1953 and at Aston Down Battle of Britain display on 19 September 1953. On 5 April 1954, MF628 was flown to Hemswell for filming of the Dam Busters, returning to St Athan on 14 October 1954. Believed to be the final flight of a Wellington was on 24 January 1955 when it was flown from St Athan to the Vickers test airfield at Wisley, flown by Flt Sgt 'Herbie' Marshall with a flight time of one hour and ten minutes.

MF628 remained in external storage at Wisley, appearing in the RAeS Garden Party on static display in July 1956. Allocated to the planned RAF Museum, it was moved under cover at Hendon in November 1957, but by late 1959, it was moved to the BEA hangar at Heathrow for some maintenance work to be carried out. In 1961, it was moved to 71 MU at Bicester for repairs and painting in preparation for storage at Biggin Hill in March 1961, where it was one of the

Wellington T 10 MF628 engine running at Wisley. (*Maurice Marsh*)

static aircraft at the annual Battle of Britain displays. Early in 1968 the aircraft was returned to St Athan for more in-depth restoration in preparation for the RAF fiftieth anniversary display at Abingdon, where it later suffered substantial damage. Following more repairs, it was stored at Henlow before finally moving the RAF Museum at Hendon in October 1971 where it was put on permanent display in camouflage colours. In the summer of 2010, it was moved to the Michael Beetham Conservation at Cosford for an in-depth restoration including a replacement of the deteriorating fabric, as well as repairs where needed, ready to be returned for display at Hendon.

In addition to two complete Wellingtons, there are also significant remains surviving of another four aircraft.

Mk I L4288 was serving with IX Squadron when it was involved in a mid-air collision with Wellington L4363 over Honington on 30 October 1939. Both aircraft crashed with the loss of the crews. The fuselage/wing centre section, engines, and nacelles and cowlings of L4288 were salvaged in 1982–1983 and now feature in the Bomber Command display at the Norfolk and Suffolk Museum at Flixton.

Mk IA L7775 flew into high ground near Braemar while on a training exercise with Lossiemouth-based 20 OTU. Surprisingly, all the crew survived and the remains were recovered in the summer of 1985 by the North Yorkshire Aircraft Recovery Centre where the gun turrets are now restored. The wings and parts of the forward fuselage are displayed at the Lincolnshire Aviation Centre at East Kirkby. Parts of the nose and tail were preserved in the Wellington Museum at Moreton-in-Marsh, wartime home for Wellington equipped 21 OTU, until 2013 when the parts were relocated to the Stratford Armouries Museum. It would be logical to reunite these parts to create a complete aircraft where the exhibit could be more appreciated.

Mk IV Z1206 ran out of fuel while flying with 104 OTU at Nutts Corner, Belfast, and was force-landed close to the beach at Uigg on the Isle of Lewis on 26 January 1944. The wreckage was washed up on the beach and became buried in the sand, but the forward fuselage was salvaged in 2002 by the Midland Aircraft Recovery Group at Kenilworth.

Mk III BK309 rear fuselage and tail in preserved in the Flyhistorisk Museum at Sola Airport, in Stavanger, Norway. It was flown by 150 Squadron on a mine-laying operation to Norway on 26 January 1944 when it crashed into a lake. Two crew were lost, but three survived to become POWs.

Wellington T 10 MF628 stored at Wisley after grounding. (*BAE Systems*)

Wellington T 10 MF628 stored at Biggin Hill being cleaned ready for a Battle of Britain air show static park. (*BAE Systems*)

Wellington T 10 MF628 in static park for RAF fiftieth anniversary royal review at Abingdon on 14 June 1968. (*Author's photo*)

Wellington T 10 MF628 at RAF fiftieth anniversary royal review at Abingdon on 14 June 1968. (*BAE Systems*)

APPENDIX I

Specifications

With the change of military mark numbers from Roman to Arabic in 1948, for post-war aircraft, Arabic numerals have been used.

B.9/32 Prototype K4049

One built, first flight 15 June 1936
   Accommodation: pilot and four or five crew members
   Powered by Bristol Pegasus X engines developing 915 hp
   Gross weight 21,000 lb
   Max speed 250 mph at 8,000 feet
   Armament (proposed): nose and tail single guns, bomb load 9 × 500-lb bombs for short range operations and 9 × 250-lb bombs for long range

B Mk I

181 built
   Accommodation: pilot and four crew members
   Wing span 86 feet, length 61 feet 3 inches, height 17 feet 5 inches
   Empty weight 18,000 lb, gross weight 24,850 lb
   Powered by Bristol Pegasus XVIII engines developing 1,050 hp
   Range 3,200 miles at 180 mph at 15,000 feet; max. speed 245 mph, service ceiling 21,600 feet
   Armament: forward and ventral gun turrets, bomb load 4,500 lb

B Mk IA

187 built
   Dimensions as Mk I
   Powered by Bristol Pegasus X. Strengthened undercarriage with larger wheels

B Mk IB

Not built

B Mk IC

2,685 built
   Accommodation: pilot and four or five crew
   Wing span: 86 feet 2 inches, length 64 feet 7 inches, height 17 feet 5 inches
   Empty weight: 18,556 lb, gross weight 28,500 lb
   Powered by Bristol Pegasus XVIII engines developing 1,050 hp
   Range 2,550 miles at 180 mph at 15,000 feet; max. speed 235 mph, service ceiling 18,000 feet
   Armament: twin-gun nose and tail turrets, plus two beam guns, bomb load 4,500 lb

B Mk II

402 built
   Accommodation: pilot and four crew
   Wing span: 86 feet 2 inches, length 64 feet 7 inches, height 17 feet 5 inches
   Empty weight: 20,258 lb, gross weight 33,000 lb
   Powered by Rolls-Royce Merlin X engines developing 1,145 hp
   Range: 2,200 miles at 180 mph at 15,000 feet; max. speed 25mph at 17,500 feet, service ceiling 23,500 feet
   Armament: twin-gun nose turret, four-gun rear turret, two beam guns, bomb load 4,000 lb

B Mk III

1,519 built
   Dimensions as Mk IC
   Powered by Bristol Hercules engines XI developing 1,590 hp
   Range: 2,200 miles with 1,550-lb bomb load or 1,540 miles with 4,000-lb bomb load

B Mk IV

220 built
   Dimensions as Mk III
   Powered by Pratt & Whitney Twin Wasp engines developing 1,050 hp
   Performance similar to Mk III

B Mk V 3

3 built
   High-altitude bomber with ceiling of 40,000 feet powered by two Bristol Hercules engines developing 1,425 hp

B Mk VI

64 built
   Accommodation: pilot and three crew
   Wing span: 86 feet 2 inches, length 61 feet 9 inches, height 17 feet 8 inches.
   Empty weight: 20,280 lb, gross weight 30,450 lb
   Powered by Rolls-Royce Merlin 60s developing 1,600 hp
   Range: 2,275 miles with 1,500-lb bomb load, max.
   Speed: 300 mph, service ceiling 38,500 feet
   Armament: remote control rear turret, bomb load 4,500 lb

B Mk VII

Prototype only powered by Rolls-Royce Merlin XX engines and used as engine test bed.

GR Mk VIII

394 built
   Accommodation: pilot and five or six crew
   Wing span: 86 feet 2 inches, length 64 feet 7 inches, height 17 feet 8 inches
   Empty weight: 21,118lb, gross weight 30,000 lb
   Powered by Bristol Pegasus XVIII engines developing 1,050 hp
   Range: 2,550 miles at 144 mph, max. speed 235 mph, service ceiling 19,000 feet
   Armament: front and rear two-gun turrets, two 420-lb depth charges, or two torpedoes and Leigh light

C Mk IX

Conversions of Mk IA for Transport Command, totals unknown; unarmed

B Mk X

3,803 built
   Wing span: 86 feet 2 inches, length 64 feet 7 inches, height 17 feet 6 inches
   Empty weight: 22,474lb, gross weight 36,500 lb
   Powered by Bristol Hercules VI or XVI developing 1,675 hp
   Range: 1,885 miles at 180 mph with 1,500 bomb load
   Max. speed 255 mph, service ceiling 22,000 feet
   Armament same as B Mk II
   Final bomber variant, with many converted to T MK 10s as post war navigation trainers

GR Mk XI

180 built
   Dimensions and performance similar to Mk X
   Powered by Bristol Hercules VI or XVI engines

GR Mk XII

58 built
   Bristol Hercules VI or XVI powered variant of GR Mk XIII

GR Mk XIII

845 built
   Accommodation: pilot and five or six crew
   Wing span: 86 feet 2 inches, length 64 feet 7 inches, height 17 feet 8 inches.
   Empty weight: 21,988lb, gross weight 31,000 lb
   Powered by Bristol Hercules XVII developing 1,735 hp
   Range: 1,750 miles, max. speed 250 mph, service ceiling 16,000 feet
   Armament: two-gun front turret and four-gun rear turret, two torpedoes and ASV Mk III

GR Mk XIV

840 built
Bristol Hercules XVII powered variant of GR Mk XII for anti-submarine operations

C Mk XV

18 conversions from B Mk IAs, redesignated from C Mk IA; unarmed

C Mk XVI

54 conversions from B Mk IC, redesignated from C Mk IC; unarmed

T Mk 17

9 conversions of GR Mk XI for radar training powered by Bristol Hercules engines; unarmed

T Mk 18

80 built powered by Bristol Hercules XVII for night fighter crew training; unarmed

T Mk 19

6 conversions from B Mk X for bomber crew training; unarmed

APPENDIX II

Production

Wellington production factories were at Weybridge, plus shadow factories at Broughton in North Wales and Squires Gate at Blackpool.

180 B Mk Is built at Weybridge: L4212–L4311, L4317–L4391, and R2699–R2703.

100 B Mk Is, IAs, and ICs built at Broughton: L7770–L7789, L7790–L7819, L7840–L7874, and L7885–L7899. Some conversions to C Mk XVI.

120 B Mk IAs built at Weybridge: 2865–N2914, N2935–N2964, and N2980–N3019. Some conversions to C Mk X.

50 B Mk IAs built at Weybridge: P2515–P2532 and P9205–P9236; plus 50 B Mk IC built at Weybridge P9237–P9250 and P9265–P9300. Some conversions to B Mk III, C Mk XV, and C Mk XVI.

550 B Mk ICs built at Broughton: R1000–R1049, R1060–R1099, R1135–R1184, R1210–R1254, R1265–R1299, R1320–R1349, R1354–R1414, R1435–R1474, R1490–R1539, R1585–R1629, R1695–R1729, and R1757–R1806. Some conversions to B Mk IV and C Mk XVI.

100 B Mk ICs built at Weybridge: R3150–R3179, R3195–R3239, and R3275–R3299. Some conversions to B Mk II, B Mk IV, and C Mk XVI.

300 B Mk ICs built at Weybridge: T2548–T2477, T2501–T2520, T2541–T2580, T2606–T2625, T2701–T2750, T2801–T2850, T2873–T2922, and T2951–T3000. Conversions to B Mk II, GR Mk VIII, and C Mk XVI.

300 Weybridge-built models, consisting of 74 B Mk ICs: W5612–W5614, W5616–W5618, W5620–W5622, W5624–W5630, W5644, W5646, W5648, W5650, W5652, W5654, W5656, W5658, W5660, W5663–W5670, W5673, W5675, W5677, W5679–W5690, W5703–W5726, and W5729.

199 B Mk IIs: W5352–W5401, W5414–W5463, W5476–W5500, W5513–W5537, and W5550–W5598.

27 GR Mk VIIIs: W5615, W5619, W5623, W5631, W5645, W5647, W5649, W5651, W5653, W5655, W5657, W5659, W5661, W5662, W5671, W5672,

W5674, W5676, W5678, W5725, W5728, and W5730–W5735. Some conversions to C Mk XVI.

1 B Mk V W5795 and 20 B Mk VIs: W5796–W5815 built at Weybridge.

500 Blackpool-built models, consisting of 50 B Mk ICs: X3160–3179 and X3192–X3221.

450 B Mk IIIs: X3222–X3226, X3275–X3289, X3304–X3313, X3330–X3374, X3387–X3426, X3445–X3489, X3538–X3567, X3584–X3608, X3633–X3677, X3694–X3728, X3741–X3754, X3784–X3823, X3855–X3890, X3923–X3957, and X3984–X4003. Conversions to B Mk X and C Mk XVI.

710 Broughton-built models, consisting of 378 B MK ICs: X9600–X9644, X9658–X9707, X9733–X9757, X9784–X9834, X9871–X9890, X9905–X9954, X9974–X9993, Z1040–Z1054, Z1066–Z1115, and Z1139–Z1181.

195 B Mk IVs: Z1182–Z1183, Z1202–Z1221, Z1243–Z1292, Z1311–Z1345, Z1375–Z1424, and Z1459–Z1496.

137 B Mk IIIs: Z1562–Z1578, Z1592–Z1626, Z1648–Z1697, and Z1717–Z1751. Some conversions to C Mk XVI.

200 Weybridge-built B Mk IIs: Z8328–Z8377, Z8397–Z8441, Z8489–Z8538, Z8567–Z8601, and Z8643–Z8662.

250 Weybridge-built B Mk ICs: Z8702–Z8736, Z8761–Z8810, Z8827–Z8871, Z8891–Z8910, Z8942–Z8991, Z9016–Z9045, and Z9095–Z9114. Some conversions to GR Mk VIII and C Mk XVI.

50 Weybridge-built B Mk ICs: AD589–AD608 and AD624–AD653.

50 Weybridge-built models, consisting of 43 B Mk ICs: BB455–BB460, BB462–BB465, BB467–BB470, BB472–BB475, BB477–BB480, BB482–BB484, BB497–BB502, BB504–BB512, and BB514–BB516.

7 GR Mk VIIIs: BB461, BB466, BB471, BB476, BB481, BB503, and BB513.

600 Broughton-built B Mk IIIs: BJ581–BJ625, BJ688–BJ730, BJ753–BJ801, BJ818–BJ847, BJ876–BJ922, BJ958–BJ991, BK123–BK166, BK179–BK214, BK234–BK281, BK295–BK315, BK330–BK358, BK385–BK408, BK425–BK471, BK489–BK517, and BK534–BK564.

150 Blackpool-built models, consisting of 145 B Mk IIIs: DF542–DF579, DF594–DF608, DF610–DF642, DF664–DF685, DF687–DF700, DF702–DF709, DF727–DF729, DF731–DF739, and DF741–DF743.

5 B Mk Xs: DF609, DF686, DF701, DF730, and DF740.

44 Weybridge-built models, consisting of 9 B Mk VIAs: DR471–DR479.

35 B Mk VIGs: DR480–DR504 and DR519–DR528.

415 B Mk ICs built at Broughton: DV411–DV458, DV473–DV522, DV536–DV579, DV593–DV624, DV638–DV678, DV694–DV740, DV757–DV786, DV799–DV846, DV864–DV898, and DV914–DV953. Some conversions to C Mk XVI.

16 Weybridge-built B Mk ICs: ES980–ES995. ES986 converted to GR Mk VIII.

1,125 Broughton-built models, consisting of 85 B Mk ICs: HD942–HD991, HE101–HE134, and HE136–HE146.

1 B Mk IIIs: HF112

242 B Mk IVs: HF121–HF155, HF167–HF208, HF220–HF252, HF264–HF312, HF329–HF363, HF381–HF422, HF446–HF495, HF513–HF545, and HF567–HF606.

789 B Mk Xs: HE147–HE184, HE197–HE244, HE258–HE306, HE318–HE353, HE365–HE398, HE 410–HE447, HE459–HE508, HE513–HE556, HE568–HE615, HE627–HE667, HE679–HE715, HE727–HE772, HE784–HE833, HE845–HE873, HE898–HE931, and HE946–HE995.

8 GR Mk XIIs: HF113–HF120.

153 Blackpool-built models, consisting of 123 B Mk IIIs: HF609–HF613, HF615–HF621, HF623–HF625, HF627–HF629, HF631–HF633, HF635–HF637, HF639–HF641, HF643–HF645, HF647–HF649, HF666–HF668, HF670–HF703, HF718, HF719, HF721, HF722, HF724, HF726–HF728, HF730, HF731, HF734, HF736–HF738, HF740 –HF742, HF744–HF746, HF748–HF750, HF752–HF754, HF756–HF758, HF760–HF762, HF764, HF791, HF792, HF794–HF796, HF798–HF802, HF806, HF807, HF809, HF810, and HF812–HF816.

27 B Mk Xs: HF614, HF622, HF626, HF630, HF634, HF638, HF642, HF646, HF650, HF669, HF723, HF725, HF729, HF732, HF735, HF739, HF743, HF747, HF751, HF755, HF759, HF763, HF793, HF797, HF805, HF808, and HF811.

3 GR Mk XI: HF720, HF803, and HF804.

84 Weybridge-built models, consisting of 62 B Mk ICs: HF829–HF837, HF839–HF849, HF851 –HF853, HF855, HF856, HF858, HF859, HF861, HF862, HF864, HF865, HF867, HF868, HF881, HF882, HF884, HF885, HF887, HF888, HF890, HF891, HF893, HF894, HF896–HF900, HF902, HF903, HF905, HF906, HF908, HF909, HF911, HF912, HF914, HF915, HF917, HF918, HF920, and HF921.

22 GR Mk VIIIs: HF828, HF838, HF850, HF854, HF857, HF860, HF863, HF866, HF869, HF883, HF886, HF889, HF892, HF895, HF901, HF904, HF907, HF910, HF913, HF916, HF919, and HF922.

300 Weybridge-built models, HX364–HX403, HX417–HX452, HX466–HX489, HX504–HX538, HX558–HX606, HX625–HX656, HX670–HX690, HX709 –HX751, and HX767–HX786, consisting of 124 B Mk IC and 176 GR Mk VIII.

850 Blackpool-built models: HZ102–HZ150, HZ173–HZ209, HZ242–HZ284, HZ299–HZ315, HZ351–HZ378, HZ394–HZ439, HZ467–HZ487, HZ513–HZ554, HZ570–HZ604, HZ633–HZ660, HZ689–HZ727, HZ752–HZ770, HZ793–HZ820, HZ862–HZ897, HZ937–HZ981, JA104–JA151, JA176–JA210, JA256–JA273, JA295–JA318, JA337–JA363, JA378–JA426, JA442–JA481, JA497–JA539, JA561–JA585, and JA618–JA645, consisting of 301 B Mk Xs, 72 GR Mk XIs, 415 GR Mk XIIIs, and 62 B Mk III.

150 Weybridge-built models: LA964–LA998, LB110–LB156, LB169–LB197, and LB213–LB251, consisting of 16 B Mk ICs and 134 GR Mk VIIIs.

1,382 Broughton-built B Mk Xs: LN157–LN189, LN221–LN248, LN261–LN303, LN317–LN353, LN369–LN409, LN423–LN458, LN481–LN516, LN529–LN571, LN583–LN622, LN633–LN676, LN689–LN723, LN736–

LN778, LN791–LN823, LN836–LN879, LN893–LN936, LN948–LN989, LP113–LP156, LP169–LP213, LP226–LP268, LP281–LP314, LP328–LP369, LP381–LP415, LP428–LP469, LP483–LP526, LP539–LP581, LP595–LP628, LP640–LP686, LP699–LP733, LP748–LP788, LP802–LP849, LP863–LP889, LP901–LP930, LP943–LP986, LR110–LR142, LR156–LR164, LR168–LR183, and LR195–LR210.

600 Blackpool-built models: ME870–ME914, ME926–ME960, ME972–ME999, MF113–MF156, MF170–MF213, MF226–MF267, MF279–MF320, MF335–MF377, MF389–MF424, MF439–MF480, MF493–MF538, MF550–MF596, MF614–MF659, MF672–MF713, and MF725–MF742, consisting of 299 B Mk Xs, 4 GR Mk XIVs, and 297 GR Mk XIII.

250 Weybridge-built models: MP502–MP549, MP562–MP601, MP615–MP656, MP679–MP724, and MP738–MP825, consisting of 50 GR Mk XIIs, 42 GR Mk XIIIs, 53 GR Mk XIVs, and 105 GR Mk XI.

27 Blackpool-built B Mk Xs: MS470–MS496.

263 Broughton-built B Mk Xs: NA710–NA754, NA766–NA811, NA823–NA870, NA893–NA937, NA949–NA997, and NB110–NB139.

296 Broughton-built GR Mk XIVs: NB767–NB783, NB796–NB841, NB853–NB896, NB908–NB952, NB964–NB999, NC112–NC160, NC164–NC209, and NC222–NC234.

500 Blackpool-built models: NC414–NC459, NC471–NC517, NC529–NC576, NC588–NC632, NC644–NC692, NC706–NC750, NC766–NC813, NC825–NC870, NC883–NC929, NC942–NC990, ND104–ND133 consisting of 90 GR Mk XIIIs, 84 GR Mk XIVs, 30 GR Mk XVIIIs, and 296 B Mk Xs.

400 Blackpool-built models: PF820–PF866, PF879–PF915, PF927–PF999, PG112–PG157, PG170–PG215, PG227–PG269, PG282–PG326, PG338–PG379, and PG392–PG422 consisting of 162 GR Mk XIVs, 30 GR Mk XVIII, and 208 B Mk Xs.

226 Blackpool built consisting of 206 B Mk X RP312–RP329, RP336–RP347, RP352–RP358, RP373–RP391, RP396–RP411, RP430–RP469, RP483–RP526, RP538–RP590, and 20 GR Mk XVIIIs: RP330–RP335, RP348–RP351, RP392–RP395, RP412–RP415, RP428, and RP429.

APPENDIX III
Service Units

Operational Squadrons

Squadron	Role	Code	Mk	Base	Dates
8	ASW	-	GR Mk XIII	Khormaksar, Aden	12.43–1.5.45 db
IX	Bomber	KA	B Mk I	Stradishall	1.39–12.39
		WS	B Mk IA	Honington	9.39–9.40
			B Mk IC		2.40–10.41
			B Mk II		3.41–8.41
			B Mk III		7.41–8.42
			B Mk IC		5.42–6.41
12	Bomber	PH	B Mk II	Binbrook	11.40–11.42
			B Mk III		8.42–11.42
14	ASW	5, CX	GR Mk XIV	Chivenor	11.44–25.5.45 db
XV	Bomber	LS	B Mk IC	Lossiemouth	11.40–5.41
24	Transport	ZK, NQ	C Mk XVI	Hendon	2.43–1.44
36	ASW	4, RW	B Mk IC	Tanjore	12.42–7.43
			GR VIII	Dhubalia & Blida	2.43–12.43
			B X		6.43–11.43
			GR XI		7.43–9.43
			GR XII		7.43–12.43
			GR XIII		7.43–12.43
			GR XIV	Reghaia	9.43–6.45
				Chivenor	26.9.44
				Benbecula	9.3.45 - 4.6.45 db
37	Bomber	FJ, LF	B Mk I	Feltwell	5.39–11.39

Appendices

			B Mk IA		10.39–8.40
			B Mk IC	Luqa	6.40–4.43
			B Mk III	Gardabia West	3.43–4.43
			B Mk X		3.43–10.44
38	B, ASW	NH, HD	B Mk I	Marham	11.38–4.40
	Coastal		B Mk IA		9.39–6.40
			B Mk IC	To Egypt 11.40	4.40–8.42
			B Mk II		8.41–10.41
			GR Mk XI		6.43–5.44
			GR Mk XII		6.43–9.43
			GR Mk XIII		9.43–1.45
			GR Mk XIV		1.45–12.46
40	Bomber	BL	B Mk IC	Wyton	11.40–2.42 db
			B Mk IC	Abu Sueir, Egypt	5.42–6.43
			B Mk III	Gardabia South	3.43–4.44
			B Mk X	El Adem East	5.43–3.45
57	Bomber	DX	B Mk IA	Feltwell	11.40–11.40
			B Mk IC		11.40–6.42
			B Mk II		7.41–11.41
			B Mk III		1.42–9.42
69	PR		GR Mk XIII	Northolt	5.44–7.8.45 db
70	Bomber	SJ	B Mk IC	Egypt	9.40–1.43
			B Mk III		1.43–11.43
			B Mk X	Garbadia West	4.43–1.45
75	Bomber	FO	B Mk I	Honington	7.39–4.40
75 (NZ)	Bomber	AA	B Mk I	Feltwell	4.40–8.40
			B Mk IA		4.40–8.40
			B Mk IC		5.40–1.42
			B Mk III	Mildenhall	1.42–11.42
93	Mines	HN	B Mk IC	Middle Wallop	3.41–7.41
99	Bomber	VF, LN	B Mk I	Mildenhall	10.38–12.39
			B Mk IA	Newmarket	9.39–4.40
			B Mk IC		3.40–2.42
			B Mk II	Waterbeach	7.41–10.41
			B Mk IC	India	10.42–5.43
			B Mk III		4.43–8.44
			B Mk X		4.43–8.44
101	Bomber	SR	B Mk IC	West Raynham	4.41–2.42
			B Mk III	Bourn	2.42–10.42
103	Bomber	PM	B Mk IC	Newton	10.40–7.42
104	Bomber	EP	B Mk II	Driffield	4.41–8.43

				B Mk X	To Luqa 14.10.41	7.43–2.45
108		Bomber		B Mk IC	Kabrit	8.41–11.42
109		Target marking	HS	B Mk IC	Boscombe Down	12.40–12.42
				B Mk I	Tempsford	7.41–9.41
				B Mk VI	Stradishall	3.42–7.42
115		Bomber	BK, KO	B Mk I	Marham	3.39–10.39
				B Mk IA		9.39–8.40
				B Mk IC		6.40–2.42
				B Mk III	To Mildenhall 24.9.42	2.42–3.43
142		Bomber	QT	B Mk II	Binbrook	11.40–10.41
				B Mk IV	Waltham	10.41–9.42
				B Mk III	To Kirmington 12.42	9.42–8.43
				B Mk X		6.43–10.44 db
148		Bomber	BS, FS	B Mk IC	Stradishall	30.4.40–20.5.40 db
				B Mk IC	Luqa	12.40–10.41
				B Mk II	Kabrit	10.41–4.42
				B Mk IC		4.42–31.12.42 db
149		Bomber	LY, OJ	B Mk I	Mildenhall	1.39–12.39
				B Mk IA		9.39–6.40
				B Mk IC		3.40–12.41
150		Bomber	JN	B Mk IA	Newton	10.40–12.40
				B Mk IC	Snaith 7.41	10.40–12.42
				B Mk III	To Kirmington 10.42	9.42–8.43
				B Mk X	To Blida 12.42	4.43–5.10.44 db
344 Free French		ASW		GR Mk XI	Dakar	11.43–11.45
				GR Mk XIII		11.43–27.11.45 db
405 RCAF		Bomber	LQ	B Mk II	Driffield To Pocklington 6.41	5.41–4.42
407 RCAF		ASW	1, 2, C1	GR Mk XI	Docking	1.43–4.43
				GR Mk XII	To Skitten 2.43	3.43–2.44
				GR Mk XIV	To Chivenor 4.43	6.43–4.6.45 db
415 RCAF		Coastal	NH	GR Mk XIII	Thorney Island	9.43–7.44
419 RCAF		Bomber	VR	B Mk IC	Mildenhall	1.42–11.42
				B Mk III	To Leeming 8.42	2.42–11.42
420 RCAF		Bomber	PT	B Mk III	Skipton-on-Swale	8.42–4.43
				B Mk X	Middleton St George	2.43–10.43
424 RCAF		Bomber	QB	B Mk III	Topcliffe	10.42–4.43
				B Mk X	To N. Africa 5.43	2.43–10.43
425 RCAF		Bomber	KW	B Mk III	Dishforth	8.42–4.43

Appendices

			B Mk X	To N. Africa 5.43	4.43–10.43
426 RCAF	Bomber	OW	B Mk III	Dishforth	10.42–4.43
			B Mk X		3.43–6.43
			GR Mk VIII		9.42–9.43
			GR Mk XIII	Protville	6.43–5.44
			GR Mk XIV	Bone	1.44–8.6.45 db
427	Bomber	ZL	B Mk III	Croft	7.11.42–3.43
428	Bomber	NA	B Mk III	Dalton	7.11.42–4.43
			B Mk X		4.43–6.43
429	Bomber	AL	B Mk III	East Moor	7.11.42–8.43
431	Bomber	SE	B Mk X	Burn	13.11.42–7.43
432	Bomber	QO	B Mk X	Skipton-on-Swale	1.5.43–11.43
			B Mk X		4.43–6.43
460	Bomber	UV	B Mk IV	Molesworth	11.41–9.42
				To Breighton 1.42	
466	Bomber	HD	B Mk II	Driffield	15.10.42–11.42
			B Mk X	To Leconfield 12.42	11.42–9.43
524	Coastal	7R	GR Mk XIII	Davidstow Moor	4.44–1.45
			GR Mk XIV	To Langham 10.44	12.44–25.5.45 db
527	Utility	WN	B Mk X	Digby	4.45–4.46
544	PR		B Mk IV	Benson	10.42–3.43
547	Coastal		GR Mk VIII	Holmsley South	10.42–5.43
			GR Mk XI	To Chivenor 4.43	5.43–11.43
			GR Mk XIII	Thorney Island	10.43–11.43
612 RAuxAF	ASW	WL, 3, 8W	GR Mk VIII	Wick	11.42–3.43
			GR Mk XIII	Davidstow Moor 4.43	3.43–3.44
			GR Mk XIV	Chivenor 5.43	6.43–9.7.45 db
621	ASW		GR Mk XIII	Port Reitz	9.43–11.45
			GR Mk XIV	Khormaksar 12.43	1.45–12.45

South African Air Force

17	Coastal		GR Mk XII	Mediterranean	5.45–9.45
26	ASW		GR Mk XI	West Atlantic	5.43–5.45
27	ASW		GR Mk XV	Mediterranean	2.45–3.45
28	Transport		C Mk IC	Mediterranean	7.43–12.43

French Navy

Flottille 2F	ASW	GR Mk XIII GR Mk XIV	West Atlantic	11.45–6.53
Flottille 23F	ASW	GR Mk XIII GR MK XIV	West Atlantic	6.53–'55
Flottille 55S	Utility	GR Mk XIII GR Mk XIV	Mediterranean	'48–'52

Royal Hellenic Air Force

13	Transport	C Mk XIII	Mediterranean	6.45–'47
355	Transport Bomber	C Mk XIII B Mk XIV	Mediterranean	1947

Training Units (OTUs)

1 OTU	Coastal		B Mk IC	Silloth/Kirkbride	11.40–7.41
3 OTU	Coastal		B Mk IC	Kinloss	5.41–29.7.41
			GR Mk VIII	Haverfordwest	6.43–4.1.44 db
5 OTU	Coastal		GR Mk XIII	Turnberry	5.44–1.8.45 db
6 OTU	Coastal	OD	GR Mk VIII	Silloth	8.43–1.9.45
			GR Mk XI		
			GR Mk XIII		
			GR Mk XIV		
7 OTU	Coastal		B Mk IC	Limavady	1.4.42–16.5.44
			GR Mk VIII		12.42–8.43
			GR Mk XI		12.42–8.43
			GR XIII		12.43–16.5.44 db
10 OTU	Bomber	EL, JL, RK, UY, ZG	B Mk X	Abingdon	6.44–10.9.46 db
11 OTU	Bomber	KJ, OP, TX	B Mk I B Mk III B Mk X	Bassingbourn Westcott	8.4.40–10.42
					10.42–18.9.45 db
12 OTU	Bomber	FQ, JP, ML	B Mk IC B Mk III B Mk X	Benson Chipping Warden	11.40–8.41
					8.41–22.6.45 db
14 OTU	Bomber	AM, GL, VB	B Mk IC B Mk III B Mk X	Cottesmore	9.42–8.43
				Market Harborough	8.43–24.6.45 db
15 OTU	Bomber	EO, FH, KK	B Mk IA B Mk IC B Mk III B Mk X B Mk XVIII	Harwell	8.4.40–7.41
				Mount Farm	25.7.41–12.2.42
				Harwell	12.2.42–15.3.44 db
16 OTU	Bomber	GA, JS, XG	B Mk IC B Mk III B Mk X	Upper Heyford	4.42–1.1.45 db

17 OTU	Bomber	AY, JG, WJ	B Mk III B Mk X	Silverstone	17.4.43–6.45
18 OTU (Polish)	Bomber	EN, VQ, XW	B Mk I B Mk III B Mk IV B Mk X	Bramcote Finningley	11.40–3.43 3.43–30.1 45 db
19 OTU	Bomber	UO, XF, ZV	B Mk III B Mk X	Kinloss	8.44–26.6.45 db
20 OTU	Bomber	AI, HJ, JM, MK, XL, YR, ZT	B Mk IA B Mk IC B Mk III B Mk X	Lossiemouth	27.5.40–17.7.45 db
21 OTU	Bomber	ED, SJ, UH	B Mk IC B Mk III B Mk X	Moreton-in-Marsh	21.1.41–25.11.46
22 OTU	Bomber	DD, LT, OX, XN	B Mk IC B Mk III B Mk X	Wellesbourne Mountford	14.4.41–24.7.45 db
23 OTU	Bomber	BY, FZ, WE	B Mk IC B Mk III B Mk X	Pershore	1.4.41–15.3.44
24 OTU	Bomber	FB, TY, UF	B Mk III B Mk X	Honeybourne	4.44–24.7.45 db
25 OTU	Bomber	PP, ZP	B Mk IC B Mk III B Mk X	Finningley	5.41–7.1.43
26 OTU	Bomber	EU, PB, WG	B Mk IC B Mk II B Mk X	Wing	2.43–4.3. 46 db
27 OTU	Bomber	BB, UJ, YL	B Mk IC B Mk III B Mk X	Lichfield	23.4.41–22.6.45 db
28 OTU	Bomber	LB, QN, WY	B Mk IC B Mk II B Mk X	Wymeswold	16.5.42–15.10.44 db
29 OTU	Bomber	NT, TF	B Mk III B Mk X B Mk XIII	North Luffenham	6.42–27.4.45 db
30 OTU	Bomber	BT, KD, TN	B Mk IC B Mk III B Mk X	Hixon Gamston	23.7.42–2.2.45 2.2.45–12.6.45 db
51 OTU	Night Fighter	BD, PF	GR Mk XI T Mk XVII T Mk XVIII	Cranfield	3.44–14.6.45 db
54 OTU	Night Fighter	BF, LX, ST, YX	B Mk X T Mk XVII, T Mk XVIII	Charterhall East Moor	2.45–1.11.45 1.11.45–1.5.47
62 OTU	Observers		T Mk XVII T Mk XVIII	Ouston	3.45–14.5.45
63 OTU	Night Fighter	HI	B Mk XI T XVII	Honiley Chedworth	9.43–21.3 44 10.43–21.3 44
76 OTU	Bomber		B Mk IC B Mk III B Mk X	Aqir	1.10.43–30.7.45
77 OTU	Bomber		B Mk IC B Mk III B Mk VIII B Mk X B Mk XIV	Qastina	1.1.44–18.6.45

78 OTU	Recce		B Mk III GR Mk VIII B Mk X GR Mk XII GR Mk XIII GR Mk XIV	Ein Shemer	1.2.44–23.7.45 db
81 OTU	Transport	EZ, JB, KG	C Mk III C Mk X	Sleap	11.44–10.8.45
82 OTU	Bomber	BZ, KA, TD, 9C	B Mk III B Mk X	Ossington	1.6.43–9.1.45 db
83 OTU	Bomber	FI, GZ, MZ	B Mk III B Mk X	Peplow	1.8.43–28.10.44 db
84 OTU	Bomber	CO, CZ, IF	B Mk III B Mk X	Desborough	1.9.43–14.6.45 db
85 OTU	Bomber	9P, 2X	B Mk III B Mk X	Husbands Bosworth	15.6.44–14.6.45 db
86 OTU	Bomber		B Mk III B Mk X	Gamston	15.6.44–15.10.44 db
104 OTU	Transport		C Mk IV	Nutts Corner	12.3.43–5.2.44 db
105 OTU	Transport	I5, 8F, 7Z	C Mk IC C Mk X	Bramcote	5.4.43–9.44
111 OTU	Recce		GR Mk XIII GR Mk XIV	Lossiemouth	1.9.45–21.5.46 db

Air Gunners Schools

1 AGS	Gunnery		B Mk III B Mk X	Pembrey	26.11.44–21.6.45 db
2 AGS	Gunnery		B Mk III B Mk X	Dalcross	18.11.44–24.11.45 db
3 AGS	Gunnery		B Mk III B Mk X	Castle Kennedy	3.45–21.6.45 db
10 AGS	Gunnery	FFA–FFD	B Mk III B Mk X	Barrow	5.45–30.6.46 db
11 AGS	Gunnery	FFE–FFG	B Mk III B Mk X GR Mk XIV	Andreas	11.44–19.9.46 db
12 AGS	Gunnery		B Mk X	Bishops Court	2.45–31.5.45 db
1 India	Gunnery		B Mk X	Bairagarh	12.5.43–1.7.45 db

Air Navigation Schools

1 ANS	Navigation	FFI–FFK	T Mk 10	Topcliffe	9.4.47–1.5.54 db
2 ANS	Navigation	FFM–FFP	T Mk 10	Bishops Court	4.6.47
				Middleton St George	1.10.47
				Thorney Island	15.5.50
5 ANS	Navigation	FFI–FFK	T Mk 10	Jurby	31.5.45
				Topcliffe	17.9.46–9.4.47

6 ANS	Navigation		T Mk 10	Litchfield	15.2.52–1.12.53
7 ANS	Navigation	FFM–FFP	T Mk 10	Bishops Court	31.5.45–4.6.47
10 ANS	Navigation	FFR–FFU	T Mk 10	Dumfries	11.6.45
				Chipping Warden Swanton Morley	10.7.45
				Driffield	1.12.45
					9.46–1.3.48 db

General Reconnaissance Units

1 GRU	Anti-mines		DW Mk I	Manston	19.12.39
				Ismailia	18.5.40–10.3.44 db
2 GRU	Anti-mines		DW Mk I	Bircham Newton	4.3.40
				Ismailia	16.5.40–6.40
3 GRU	Anti-mines		DW Mk I	Manston	22.4.40
				Thorney Island	24.5.40–26.7.40 db

Advanced Flying Schools

201 AFS	Crew Training	FMA & FMB	T Mk 10	Swinderby	15.3.47–10.51
202 AFS	Crew Training	FME	T Mk 10	Finningley	15.3.47–1.12.47 db

Ferry Training Units

301 FTU	Ferry Crews		B Mk IC	Lyneham	1.44–3.44
303 FTU	Ferry Crews		B Mk IA/C GR Mk VIII B Mk X GR Mk XIII GR Mk XIV	Stornoway	15.12.42–5.3.43
				Talbenny	5.3.43–8.9.44 db
304 FTU	Ferry Crews		B Mk IC	Melton Mowbray	1.12.43–15.1.44
310 FTU	Ferry Crews		B Mk II B Mk X	Harwell	30.4.43–17.12 43
311 FTU	Ferry Crews		B Mk I B Mk III B Mk X	Moreton-in-Marsh	1.5.43–1.5 44 db

(Transport Support) Conversion Units

1380 CU	Support Crews	EZ, JB, KG	B Mk X	Tilstock	10.8.45–21.1.46 db
1381 CU	Transport Support	I5, 8F, 7Z	C Mk X	Bramcote	10.8.45–11.45
1692 TU	Bomber Support	4X	T Mk XVIII	Great Massingham	12.44–16.6.45 db

General Reconnaissance Units

1 GRU	Anti-mines		DW Mk I	Manston	3.40–18.5.40
				Ismailia	22.5.40–10.3.44 db
2 GRU	Anti-mines		DW Mk I	Bircham Newton	4.3.40 -16.5.40
				Ismailia	22.5.40–6.40
3 GRU	Anti-mines		DW Mk I	Manston	22.4.40–24.5.40
				Thorney Island	24.5.40–26.7.40 db

Middle East Training Schools

2 METS	Crew training		B Mk IC B Mk II B Mk III	Kabrit	15.4.42–10.42
3 METS	Crew training		B Mk IC	Amman	23.3.42–15.11.44 db
4 METS	Crew training		B Mk IC	Kabrit	1.5.42–20.3.43
				Ramat David	20.3.43–10.5.43
5 METS	Anti-shipping	5-A, 5-B etc	B Mk IC	Shallufa	16.5.42–7.11.43
			GR Mk VIII		

Torpedo Training Units

TTU	Torpedo		GR Mk VIII	Turnberry	11.42–1.1.43
1 TTU	Torpedo		GR Mk XIII	Turnberry	1.1.43–22.5.44
			GR Mk XIV		
			GR Mk XIII		1.8.45–10.12.47 db
			GR Mk XIV		

Flying Refresher Schools

FRS	Crew training	N, O	T Mk 10	Finningley	1.6.49–1.4.51
101 FRS	Crew training	N, O	T Mk 10	Finningley	1.4.51 -1.2.52 db

Note: db—disbanded

Among other training and development units was the following:

No. 1 ASV Training Centre, Aircraft Delivery Unit, Coastal Command Development Unit, Air-Sea Warfare development Unit, Central Navigation School, Central Navigation & Control School, Empire Air Navigation School, Central Gunnery School, No. 1 Air Armament School, Bomber Command Instructional School, No. 2 School of General Reconnaissance, Central Flying School, No. 228 Operational Conversion Unit, No. 9 Ferry Pilots Pool, Marine Aircraft Experimental Establishment, Aeroplane & Armament Experimental Establishment, Royal Aircraft Establishment, Air Fighting Development Unit, Signals Flying Unit, and No. 1 Radar Training School.

Further Reading

Bond S., *Wimpy* (Grub Street 2014)
Bowyer C., *The Wellington* (William Kimber, 1986)
Bowyer C., *Wellington at War* (Ian Allan, 1982)
Chorlton M., 'Vickers Wellington', *Aeroplane* (2014)
Ellis K., 'Wellington', *FlyPast*
Jefford Wg Cdr C. G., 'RAF Squadrons', *Airlife* (1988)
Lumsden A., *Wellington Special* (Ian Allan)
Sturtivant R., Hamlin J., and Halley J., *RAF Flying Training & Support Units* (Air Britain, 1997)
Wells K., *A Village Airfield at War* (Egon, 1993)